YORK NOTES

# KING LEAR

## WILLIAM SHAKESPEARE

**Notes by Rebecca Warren
Revised by Michael Sherborne**

D1341671

PEARSON

YORK
PRESS

The right of Rebecca Warren to be identified as Author of this Work
has been asserted by her in accordance with the Copyright,
Designs and Patents Act 1988

YORK PRESS
322 Old Brompton Road, London SW5 9JH

PEARSON EDUCATION LIMITED
Edinburgh Gate, Harlow,
Essex CM20 2JE, United Kingdom
Associated companies, branches and representatives throughout the world

First published 1998
New edition 2003
This new and fully revised edition 2015

10 9 8 7 6 5 4 3

ISBN: 978–1–4479–8224–1

Illustration on page 49 by Alan Batley
Phototypeset by Border Consultants
Printed in China by Golden Cup

Photo credits: Studio-Annika/Thinkstock for page 6 bottom / © iStock/soloarseven for page 8 bottom / © iStock/stockcam for page 9 middle / Valery Sidelnykov/Shutterstock for page 11 bottom / Dudaeva/Shutterstock for page 12 bottom / © iStock/© DianaHirsch for page 15 bottom / Jacqui Martin/Shutterstock for page 16 middle / Marbury/Shutterstock for page 17 bottom / Culture Club/Getty for page 18 bottom / Popkov/Shutterstock for page 19 top / Ruslan Guzov/Shutterstock for page 20 bottom / © iStock/lionvision for page 21 top / Daria Vorontsova/Shutterstock for page 22 middle / turtix/Shutterstock for page 23 top / © iStock/ironrodart for page 24 middle / Zacharias Pereira da Mata/Shutterstock for page 26 middle / © iStock/AlexD75 for page 27 bottom / Africa Studio/Shutterstock for page 28 middle / FXQuadro/Shutterstock for page 29 middle / © iStock/Cornelia Schaible for page 30 bottom / Kiseley Andrey Valarevich/Shutterstock for page 31 bottom / vladimir salman/Shutterstock for page 33 bottom / vladimir salman/Shutterstock for page 34 bottom / © iStock/MLiberra for page 35 top / Carmelka/Thinkstock for page 37 bottom / Fernando Cortes/Shutterstock for page 38 bottom / Platslee/Shutterstock for page 39 bottom / phodo/Shutterstock for page 41 top / LockStockBob/Shutterstock for page 42 middle / © iStock/alexovicsattila for page 43 top / Ivonne Wierink/Shutterstock for page 45 bottom / antb/Shutterstock for page 46 bottom / Fuse/Thinkstock for page 48 bottom / Ruslan Guzov/Shutterstock for page 50 top / Tomnamon/Shutterstock for page 50 bottom / Dudaeva/Shutterstock for page 52 top / Daria Vorontsova/Shutterstock for page 52 middle / © iStock/ © Spiritartist for page 52 bottom / Valery Sidelnykov/Shutterstock for page 54 top / © iStock/OlgaMitsova for page 54 bottom / vladimir salman/Shutterstock for page 56 top / focal point/Shutterstock for page 56 bottom / mentona/Thinkstock for page 57 bottom / FXQuadro/Shutterstock for page 58 top / Imaake/Shutterstock for page 59 bottom / © iStock/DianaHirsch for page 60 top / Georgy Kurvatov/Shutterstock for page 60 bottom / © iStock/DianaHirsch for page 61 bottom / © iStock/AlexD75 for page 62 top / © iStock/AnnBaldwin for page 62 bottom / © iStock/Alessandro di Noia for page 63 top / Sinelev/Shutterstock for page 64 top / lero/Shutterstock for page 65 top / Fernando Cortes/Shutterstock for page 66 middle / Aksenova Natalya/Shutterstock for page 68 top / gallimaufry/Shutterstock for page 69 bottom / © iStock/dem10 for page 71 top / littleny/Shutterstock for page 73 bottom / Andrey Burmakin/Shutterstock for page 75 top / italianestro/Shutterstock for page 77 top / Natali Glado/Shutterstock for page 78 bottom / wassily-architect/Shutterstock for page 79 bottom / The Print Collector/Alamy for page 81 bottom / Padmayogini/Shutterstock for page 83 middle / Matt Gibson/Shutterstock for page 84 middle / © WENN Ltd/Alamy page 85 middle / murengstockphoto/Shutterstock for page 86 top / De Agostini/Getty for page 87 bottom / Algol/Shutterstock for page 88 bottom / wavebreakmedia/Shutterstock for page 105 middle

# CONTENTS

# PART FIVE: CONTEXTS AND INTERPRETATIONS

# PART SIX: PROGRESS BOOSTER

# PART SEVEN: FURTHER STUDY AND ANSWERS

## HOW TO STUDY *KING LEAR*

These York Notes can be used in a range of ways to help you read, study and revise for your exam or assessment.

## Become an informed and independent reader

Throughout the Notes, you will find the following key features to aid your study:

- **'Key context'** margin features: these will help to widen your knowledge of the setting, whether historical, social or political. They are highlighted by the AO3 (Assessment Objective 3) symbol to remind you of the connection to aspects you may want to refer to in your exam responses.
- **'Key interpretation'** boxes (a key part of AO5): do you agree with the perspective or idea that is explained here? Does it help you form your own view on events or characters? Developing your own interpretations is a key element of higher level achievement in A Level, so make use of this and similar features.
- **'Key connection'** features (linked to AO4): whether or not you refer to such connections in your exam writing, having a wider understanding of how the play, or aspects of it, links to other texts or ideas, can give you new perspectives on the text.
- **'Study focus'** panels: these help to secure your own understanding of key elements of the text. Being able to write in depth on a particular point, or explain a specific feature, will help your writing sound professional and informed.
- **'Key quotation'** features: these identify the effect of specific language choices – you could use these for revision purposes at a later date.
- **'Progress booster'** features: these offer specific advice about how to tackle a particular aspect of your study, or an idea you might want to consider discussing in your exam responses.
- **'Extract analysis'** sections: these are vital for you to use either during your reading, or when you come back to the text afterwards. These sections take a core extract from a chapter and explore it in real depth, explaining its significance and impact, raising questions, and offering interpretations.

## Stay on track with your study and revision

Your first port of call will always be your teacher, and you should already have a good sense of how well you are doing, but the Notes offer you several ways of measuring your progress.

- **'Revision task'**: throughout the Notes, there are some challenging, but achievable, written tasks for you to do relevant to the section just covered. Suggested answers are supplied in **Part Seven**.
- **'Progress check'**: this feature comes at the end of **Parts Two** to **Five**, and contains a range of short and longer tasks which address key aspects of the Part of the Notes you have just read. Below this is a grid of key skills which you can complete to track your progress, and rate your understanding.
- **'Practice task'** and **'Mark scheme'**: use these features to make a judgement on how well you know the text and how well you can apply the skills you have learned.

**The text used in these Notes is the Heinemann Advanced edition, 2000.**

---

**A02 PROGRESS BOOSTER**

You can choose to use the Notes as you wish, but as you read the play, it can be useful to read over the **Part Two** summaries and analysis in order to embed key events, ideas and developments in the narrative.

**A02 PROGRESS BOOSTER**

Don't forget to make full use of **Parts Three** to **Five** of the Notes during your reading of the play. You may have essays to complete on genre, or key themes, or on the impact of specific settings, and can therefore make use of these in-depth sections. Or you may simply want to check out a particular idea or area as you're reading or studying the play in class.

**A01 PROGRESS BOOSTER**

**Part Six: Progress Booster** will introduce you to different styles of question and how to tackle them; help you to improve your expression so that it has a suitably academic and professional tone; assist you with planning and use of evidence to support ideas, and, most importantly, show you three sample exam responses at different levels with helpful AO-related annotations and follow-up comments. Dedicating time to working through this Part will be time you won't regret.

# *KING LEAR*: A SNAPSHOT

## A powerful drama

*King Lear* tells the story of an elderly ruler in pagan Britain who submits his daughters to a love-test and then suffers the consequences as his life, family and nation are torn apart by his fatal error of judgement. The play explores many human issues: the conflict between parents and children, sibling rivalry, mental health, friendship and disloyalty, the painful process of working out who and what you are. This play is a stark but dramatically exhilarating examination of family conflict, political instability and the ageing process. Under pressure of events, characters are forced to change their loyalties or even identities from scene to scene. All the deaths that occur – on and off stage – are violent and brutal.

## Shakespeare's greatest tragedy?

For many critics this is Shakespeare's most profound **tragedy**, one of the greatest plays ever written and one which throws up perplexing questions. Is human nature essentially cruel or kind? How do we assess justice? What comfort can we draw from religion? There are no easy answers to these questions, or to the many others you will find yourself asking as you study the play. *King Lear* is a disturbing read which pushes its readers, as its central character is pushed, to confront the nature of suffering and the human condition. *King Lear* also offers many opportunities to experience the two emotions Aristotle defined as necessary for tragedy: pity and fear.

## An ancient story

The story of a king who submits his three daughters to a love-test and rejects the youngest and truest is an ancient folk tale, related to the story of Cinderella. Shakespeare probably knew it from various retellings: in the historian Holinshed's *Chronicles,* Edmund Spenser's poem *The Faerie Queen,* John Higgins's *A Mirror for Magistrates* and a play of the 1590s, *The True Chronicle History of King Leir.* Shakespeare adds a **subplot** – the story of Gloucester and his sons – which heightens the tragedy that occurs in the **main plot** and provides points of comparison. Shakespeare probably found this subplot in Sir Philip Sidney's prose romance *Arcadia.* Sidney tells the story of a blind king with two sons, one of whom plots against him. When he realises the truth about his evil son, the king wishes to throw himself from a cliff.

Shakespeare may also have been familiar with two 'real life' Lear stories. In the 1580s a former mayor of London, Sir William Allen, divided his property between his three daughters, but was badly treated by them. Then in 1603 the eldest daughter of Sir Brian Annesley and her husband tried to have him certified as a senile lunatic, so that they could take control of his property. His youngest daughter Cordell saved the day by challenging her sister in court.

By considering Shakespeare's changes and additions to the Lear story and his use of the Gloucester subplot, it is possible to see where the playwright's dramatic interests lie. Lear's breakdown is Shakespeare's invention, as is the manner of Cordelia's death. It seems that Shakespeare was determined to produce an impression of bleakness.

# Textual problems

*King Lear* was probably written between late 1605 and early 1606. The first published version (the First Quarto), which appeared in 1608, is full of errors. It seems to have been produced by an inexperienced printer, perhaps using a rough draft of the play. After the playwright's death, all of Shakespeare's works were prepared for publication as the First Folio of 1623.

The Folio version, which is much more accurate, may have been based in part on a prompt book copy of *King Lear*. However, it is likely that this shorter text gives us a later, revised version of the play, as the Quarto and Folio texts of *King Lear* differ quite radically. The Quarto omits approximately a hundred lines which are found in the Folio, while the Folio does not include three hundred lines of the Quarto. The main omissions in the Folio include Lear's 'mock trial' of Goneril in the hovel during Act III, the sympathetic dialogue between Cornwall's two servants following Gloucester's blinding, and all of Act IV Scene 3 where the Gentleman describes Cordelia's grief. The end of the final scene of the play, including Lear's final speech, is also different in the two texts.

# One play or two?

Which version of the play most closely reflects Shakespeare's dramatic intentions? It is very difficult to say. The Quarto version is highly unreliable, but we cannot be sure that Shakespeare himself made the revisions found in the Folio. Some scholars point out that to combine both versions produces a text which is certainly not what Shakespeare intended; others think that such a conflated version gives the fullest access to Shakespeare's achievement. Most stage performances draw on both texts. For a more detailed discussion of the Quarto and Folio versions of *King Lear*, see R. A. Foakes's introduction to the play in the Arden edition, and Stanley Wells and Gary Taylor's edition of *The Complete Works*. Check which version(s) of *King Lear* your own play text is based on. The decision will affect which material is included and also the line and scene numbers.

The edition used in these Notes, the Heinemann Advanced *King Lear* edited by Frank Green (second edition, 2000), is based on the Folio with the additional missing lines from the Quarto restored.

**A03** **KEY CONTEXT**

Shakespeare's company performed *King Lear* for King James I on St Stephen's Night in 1606. St Stephen's Night, which we now call Boxing Day, was traditionally associated with hospitality to the poor and homeless. A play in which a sovereign is himself reduced to a beggar might be considered an apt choice for such a royal performance. For a detailed discussion of this historical context, see Leah Marcus's essay 'Retrospective: *King Lear* on St Stephen's Night, 1606' in *New Casebooks: King Lear*, ed. Kiernan Ryan, 1993.

## **A02**

## Study focus: Key issues to explore

As you study the text and revise for the exam, keep in mind these key elements and ideas:

- The shifting sympathy we feel for the characters as the story unfolds
- The justice or injustice of each character's eventual fate
- The nature of Lear's tragedy
- The way the subplot of Gloucester and his sons gives dramatic support to the story of Lear and his daughters
- The role of the Fool
- The **symbolism** of blindness and sight
- The relevance of the gods
- The conflicting views of nature held by the characters
- The significance of the key word 'Nothing'

In each case, make sure you develop your own interpretations and prepare yourself with the help of these Notes to argue your viewpoint on them.

## SYNOPSIS

### Act I: Fatal misjudgements

**KEY INTERPRETATION**

In *Reading Shakespeare in Performance: King Lear*, 1991, James Lusardi and June Schlueter compare in detail the staging and acting choices made in two television versions of *King Lear*, Jonathan Miller's 1982 production featuring Michael Hordern and Michael Elliott's 1983 version featuring Laurence Olivier. In the latter production, for example, the first scene features a slow procession into a temple like Stonehenge, Lear entering last wearing a crown and a robe to emphasise his importance as a king and a priest. In the 1982 production a bareheaded Lear leads the royal family into a plain room, minimising his kingly role and instead stressing his place as the father of an aristocratic household.

Wishing for a quiet life without responsibilities, the elderly King Lear decides to divide his kingdom between his three daughters, Goneril, Regan and Cordelia. He devises a love-test to see which daughter loves him most, expecting his favourite youngest daughter Cordelia to 'win' and claim the largest share of the kingdom. Cordelia thwarts his plan by refusing to take part. Furious, Lear casts her off, banishing the Duke of Kent when he tries to intervene, and divides the kingdom between Goneril and Regan. Cordelia marries the King of France and leaves Britain. Kent later returns in disguise and persuades Lear to employ him as one of his followers.

Meanwhile, Lear's friend the Earl of Gloucester is treated treacherously by his illegitimate son Edmund, who dupes him into believing that his legitimate son Edgar seeks his life. Goneril and Regan start to plot against their father, too. Lear intends to live with each of his favoured daughters in turn, but a quarrel soon develops with Goneril. When she demands a drastic cut in the number of his followers, Lear sends Kent to inform Regan that he is moving in with her. Lear's Fool makes scathing jokes about the harm that the King has done to himself. Lear begins to worry that he is losing his mind.

### Act II: Insult and rejection

Unwilling to receive Lear, Regan and her husband the Duke of Cornwall withdraw to Gloucester's house, where they befriend Edmund. Edmund has managed to convince his father to have Edgar hunted down and killed. However, Edgar escapes his pursuers by disguising himself as Poor Tom, an unstable beggar. Kent arrives at Gloucester's house in pursuit of Regan, but finds that Goneril's disrespectful steward, Oswald, is there too. Kent insults and attacks him, and is then rude to Regan and Cornwall. Instead of asking Lear to punish Kent, they put him in the stocks – a calculated insult to the king. When Lear arrives at the house, Regan makes him wait for her and shows him little sympathy. She is then joined by Goneril. The two sisters strip their father of his power, reduce him to tears and drive him out into a fearsome storm.

### Act III: In the storm

Alone on the heath except for his faithful servants Kent and the Fool, Lear suffers a mental breakdown, ranting at the elements and acting out his feelings in fantasy. Eventually the three men take refuge in a hovel where they find Edgar disguised as Poor Tom. Gloucester tracks Lear down and arranges to have him taken to Dover, where Cordelia is going to return to Britain with the French army in order to support her father. To punish Gloucester for helping Lear, Regan and Cornwall blind him, taunting him with Edmund's treachery. One of Cornwall's servants tries to stop Gloucester's mutilation and, although Regan kills him, he wounds his master fatally.

## Act IV: Partial rescue

Still in disguise, Edgar comes upon his blinded father and leads him towards Dover. Gloucester intends to kill himself by jumping from a cliff, but Edgar tricks him into believing that he has a charmed life which makes suicide impossible. They meet with Lear, whose disturbed speeches contain bitter reflections on social and moral justice. Cordelia has sent her soldiers to find Lear, intending to restore him to the throne, but he runs from them.

Meanwhile, Goneril's husband the Duke of Albany has realised how evil his wife is and turned against her; she in turn hopes to dispose of him and marry Edmund. Edgar kills Goneril's steward Oswald, who was trying to murder Gloucester for reward money. He finds Oswald is carrying incriminating letters from both sisters. Lear and Cordelia are at last reunited at the French camp in Dover. Although still confused, Lear has learned humility and regret. Yet his reconciliation with Cordelia is threatened by an impending battle between the two armies.

## Act V: Tragic outcomes

The French army loses. Lear and Cordelia are imprisoned by Edmund, who sends a death warrant after them. However, Albany now takes charge of the British forces. Having received from Edgar the letter which shows that Goneril and Edmund were plotting to kill him, he accuses them of treason and places Edmund under arrest. Edgar, his face concealed, challenges Edmund to a fight and mortally wounds him before disclosing his true identity. The desperate Goneril poisons Regan and then kills herself. Edgar explains that he eventually revealed his true identity to Gloucester, but his father was so overcome that he died.

Kent now arrives and asks to see Lear. Edmund, hoping to do some good before his death, admits he has ordered the murder of Lear and Cordelia. He himself is carried off to die. Before his death warrant can be repealed, Lear enters carrying Cordelia's dead body. He has killed the man who hanged her but was unable to save her life. Her death is too much for Lear, even though he has come to a greater understanding of himself and others through his suffering. He dies a broken man, but perhaps believing that Cordelia has begun to revive. Albany offers the crown to Kent and Edgar, but Kent declines, his mind on his own death. Edgar becomes the new king.

**A03  KEY CONNECTION**

Other classic performances preserved for us on film are Richard Eyre's 1998 production featuring Ian Holm and Trevor Nunn's 2007 production featuring Ian McKellen. Try to see several productions of *King Lear*, best of all on stage, to get an idea of the different ways that the play can be performed.

**A03  KEY CONTEXT**

Many people have found the play's tragic conclusion almost unbearable. From 1681 to 1838 Shakespeare's version of *King Lear* was replaced on stage by Nahum Tate's rewrite, which ended with Cordelia marrying Edgar, while Lear, Kent and Gloucester all contemplated a happy retirement together.

# ACT I SCENE 1

## Summary

- As they arrive for an important meeting at the British court, the Earl of Gloucester introduces the Duke of Kent to his illegitimate son, Edmund, who is visiting him after nine years abroad. Gloucester says that he loves Edmund as much as his legitimate son, yet he talks lewdly about his conception and calls him a 'whoreson' (line 23).
- At the meeting, the elderly King Lear announces that he wants to rid himself of the cares of state, while keeping the title and status of a king. He will use a love-test to divide the kingdom between his three daughters. His two elder daughters flatter him outrageously, but his favourite youngest daughter Cordelia, to whom he had intended to give the largest share, refuses to take part, saying she loves him just as her duty requires.
- Furious, Lear banishes Cordelia and also Kent when he tries to intervene on her side. The kingdom is divided between Lear's elder daughters, Goneril and Regan.
- Lacking a dowry, Cordelia is rejected by the Duke of Burgundy. However, the King of France is happy to marry such a 'precious maid' (line 258). She leaves Britain with him.
- Meanwhile, Goneril and Regan, disturbed by their father's 'unruly' temperament (line 297), start to plot against him.

## Analysis

### Setting the scene

A mood of uncertainty is established in the first six lines, which set the scene and introduce key themes and ideas. We learn that inheritance and property issues are at stake when Kent and Gloucester discuss the division of the kingdom. Ideas about favouritism are also introduced in the opening exchange.

Edmund's silence is significant. It is symbolic of his position as the bastard son, who has no 'voice', rights or position in society. It also means that Shakespeare can keep Edmund's true character concealed at this point, so that his opening **soliloquy** in the next scene is exciting and surprising. Edmund's polite exterior conceals his evil nature, suggesting that the difference between appearances and reality is a key theme in this play. Gloucester takes his control of Edmund for granted, shown by the brief, even brutal lines he speaks about Edmund's past and future. Gloucester jokes easily about Edmund's bastardy, suggesting that he has rather lax morals. Questions about family relationships are raised here and these prepare us for the conflicts within Lear's family too.

### A foolish king

Lear's entrance is impressive, suggesting his power. But we question his use of that power almost immediately. His love-test is foolish and self-regarding, as is his desire to be treated as an important royal personage after he has given away his kingdom. We should also be alarmed by Lear's intention to break up his state. His actions are not those of a responsible ruler. In Act I Scene 1, Lear shows many times that he is most concerned with appearances, and does not see clearly. He is fooled by Goneril's and Regan's superficial speeches and fails to recognise Cordelia's and Kent's honesty.

---

**KEY CONTEXT** **A03**

Inheritance issues were a matter of national concern for Shakespeare's audience in the late sixteenth and early seventeenth centuries. Elizabeth I had been unmarried and childless, creating a fear of civil war at her death. The new king, James I of England, also James VI of Scotland, wanted to unite his two territories into one British kingdom. In the light of these developments, Lear's decision to divide Britain into three would have struck many in the audience as the height of folly.

---

**KEY INTERPRETATION** **A05**

The critic Frank Kermode argues that, because Lear has already decided how to divide up the kingdom, the only point of the love-test is for Lear to enjoy his daughters' elaborate praise. In this context Cordelia's substitution of plainness and understatement feels to him like a calculated insult. 'The rage of the King confirms that he cannot be temperate in the absence of ceremony; the love he seeks is the sort that can be offered in formal and subservient expressions, and he therefore rejects the love of Cordelia and of Kent.' (See Frank Kermode, *Shakespeare's Language*, 2000.)

---

### Two rebels: Cordelia and Kent

Cordelia epitomises honesty and genuine feeling when she says that some of her love should go to her husband when she marries. Her strength of character and integrity are shown again when she scorns Burgundy and parts frostily from her sisters. However, some commentators see Lear's youngest daughter as stubborn and destructive (like her father?).

Kent also displays subversive behaviour in this scene. He uses insulting language when he refers to Lear as 'thou' and 'old man' (line 145). However, we understand that Cordelia and Kent have Lear – and Britain's – best interests at heart. They hope to alert Lear to his false, materialistic values.

## Study focus: Lear, fearsome or pitiful? **A02**

Lear behaves like a tyrant in Act I Scene 1. However, we know he has lost control when he goes to attack Kent. He continues to issue orders, and speaks very cruelly to Cordelia, but he does so because his authority has been publicly denied. It is possible to feel some sympathy for the king in spite of his rash behaviour; at his age, his judgement may be clouded by senile dementia. He clearly loves his youngest daughter a great deal, dividing the kingdom so that she would receive the most opulent share, hoping he could rely on her 'kind nursery' (line 123) as he 'crawls' (line 40) towards death (his language here suggests the vulnerability of a baby). He is humiliated by Cordelia's refusal to take part in his love-test.

Nonetheless, we are likely to recognise the truth of Goneril's and Regan's remarks about their father at the end of the scene. They sum up the explosive, violent Lear we have just seen. Yet we should ask ourselves whether we can trust the older sisters. Perhaps Goneril and Regan simply justify the wicked intentions they already possess when they decide to 'hit together' (lines 302–3). By the end of this scene, family and national harmony have been destroyed. One daughter has challenged her father, and two more prepare to subvert his authority. We can argue that Lear's **tragic** fall proceeds from his misuse of power in Act I Scene 1. What is your assessment of Lear at this stage of the play?

**A03** **KEY CONTEXT**

In Shakespeare's day, 'thou' was the pronoun used to address close friends and children. 'You' was the polite, respectful form. Kent is therefore being disrespectful when he addresses Lear as 'thou'. Why do you think he chooses to use this pronoun?

**A05** **KEY INTERPRETATION**

Northrop Frye has pointed out that anyone unfamiliar with the story is likely to view this scene with confused sympathies, judging Lear and Gloucester to be selfish, gullible old fools, and feeling sorry for Goneril and Regan. Like Lear himself, the audience has yet to learn the shocking difference between appearance and reality.

## Key quotation: Cordelia's refusal **A01**

When Lear asks Cordelia what she can say to earn his favour, she replies, 'Nothing, my lord' (line 86), and he retorts, 'Nothing will come of nothing' (line 89).

Cordelia may seem harsh in refusing to express affection for her father on this important occasion, but she is making a protest at the complacency and poor judgement which have led him to divide and imperil the kingdom. She has the natural love of a child for her parent and believes her father should recognise this without the kind of slick flattery offered by her sisters. By rejecting Cordelia's truthfulness, Lear begins the destruction of his world and his identity. The word 'nothing' will recur in the play **ironically** as he is stripped of his power, wealth and even reason.

# ACT I SCENES 2–3

## Summary

- Edmund asks why he should be denied property and power because he is illegitimate. He declares nature to be his goddess, believing his natural qualities will let him gain advantage over his brother Edgar.

- Edmund pretends to his father that he is hiding a letter. The letter is a forgery in which 'Edgar' seems to suggest that he wishes his father dead so that he and Edmund can enjoy half of Gloucester's revenue each. Appalled, Gloucester wants Edgar arrested, but Edmund suggests he should hear Edgar condemn himself out of his own mouth before taking action. Gloucester agrees to let Edmund arrange this.

- Gloucester then reflects pessimistically on the conflict in the nation, referring to many predictions of discord. He promises Edmund that he will gain by uncovering Edgar's villainy.

- Once alone, Edmund rejects his father's superstitious beliefs, saying people are responsible for their own actions. Edmund tells Edgar that he has offended their father and suggests that he goes into hiding at Edmund's lodgings.

- Lear is now staying with Goneril. She complains to her steward Oswald about Lear and his followers, telling him to put on a 'weary negligence' (line 13) towards them. She wants to provoke a clash with her father. She intends to write to Regan to encourage her to do the same.

## Analysis

### Study focus: Plot and subplot

**A02**

Be sure to keep careful track of the similarities and contrasts as the plot and subplot unfold. Edmund's **soliloquy** at the beginning of Act I Scene 2 reveals his discontent. His last line expresses a rousing defiance: 'Now gods stand up for bastards' (line 22). Edmund is a master manipulator who takes his father and brother in with disturbing ease. Gloucester's swift rejection of Edgar mirrors Lear's rejection of Cordelia in the previous scene, while Edmund's villainy prepares the way for Goneril and Regan's treachery in the next Act. The **subplot** mirrors the Lear plot in other ways, too. Gloucester is taken in by false words and appearances, just as Lear was, and inheritance issues are again revealed as troublesome. Another innocent and virtuous child is cast off, while the father promises property to his unworthy offspring in return for a show of affection. Gloucester puts himself in his son Edmund's power, just as Lear resigned his authority to Goneril and Regan.

### Goneril's complaints

How seriously should we take Goneril's complaints about Lear and his knights in Act I Scene 3? It depends partly on how a director chooses to portray the knights in the next scene. It is also worth considering that, as Lear's host, Goneril has a duty to protect her father and behave graciously towards him. Instead, she prepares to subvert his authority. Throughout this scene her tone is assertive and uncompromising; she insists that she is the wronged party, suggesting that the balance of power is shifting from Lear to his daughters.

---

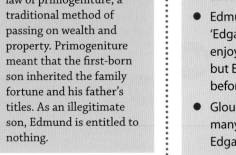

# ACT I SCENE 4

## Summary

- Kent returns in disguise as a serving man and asks Lear for employment. He earns Lear's favour by tripping up the insolent Oswald and driving him away.
- The Fool, Lear's jester, tries to make Lear realise how foolish he has been.
- Goneril accuses Lear of encouraging bad behaviour in his followers and demands that he reduce their number. Lear curses her and announces he will go to live with Regan.
- Goneril's husband, Albany, is bewildered and uneasy about what has happened, but does not assert himself.
- After Lear has gone, Goneril sends Oswald to Regan with a letter, describing the course she has taken and asking for her sister's support.

## Analysis

### Lear loses power

Lear's followers are a symbol of Lear's might and importance, but they also represent real fighting power. With only the support of a few old men, Lear will not be able to assert himself. His threats and curses seem increasingly empty as the scene unfolds. His speeches become increasingly disjointed as he becomes more distressed, hinting at the 'madness' to come.

## Study focus: Lear loses control **(A02)**

Lear finds his expectations and beliefs thwarted at every turn. He is challenged directly by Goneril; Oswald tells him that he is simply his mistress's father. The Fool's scathing jests also suggest Lear's powerlessness, as does the king's frantic to-ing and fro-ing at the end of the scene.

Swinging between curses and weeping, Lear seems to have lost his emotional self-possession. He himself begins to question his identity when he asks 'Who is it that can tell me who I am?' (line 228). His use of 'I' is at odds with the royal 'we' he invokes in his earlier question, 'Are you our daughter?' (line 217). Lear thinks – or hopes – that he is being sarcastic when he asks these questions, but the audience will recognise that they raise serious concerns. There is, however, an indication that he realises he has behaved unwisely when he says, 'Woe, that too late repents' (line 256) and calls out in anguish, 'O Lear, Lear, Lear! / Beat at this gate, that let thy folly in, / And thy dear judgement out!' (lines 269–70).

Do you feel any pity for Lear at this stage? Keep a record of how your feelings towards him change as the play progresses.

### Goneril's emergence

Goneril and Albany's different responses to Lear may hint that they will clash later in the play. Goneril is certainly more assertive than her husband at this point, and confides in her steward rather than him. She has assumed control in the **main plot** in the same ruthless way that Edmund deals with his father and brother in the subplot.

**(A03) KEY CONTEXT**

It has been suggested that the same actor originally played the Fool and Cordelia. This would explain why the two characters do not appear in the same scenes. Although doubling of this kind was common in Shakespeare's day, it would be a huge challenge for a young actor capable of playing a princess to also take on the comic part of the Fool.

**(A02) PROGRESS BOOSTER**

When analysing a scene from the play, it is important to remember that it exists as part of the unfolding drama. Be prepared to refer back to earlier scenes and forward to later ones in order to examine the scene's dramatic impact. Lear's anguished behaviour in this scene is significant because it contrasts markedly with his absolute power in Act I Scene 1 and helps us to understand, and believe in, his later breakdown.

# ACT I SCENE 5

## Summary

- Lear sends Kent to deliver a letter to Regan, announcing his arrival.
- The Fool continues to make barbed comments about Lear's predicament.
- Lear realises he has wronged Cordelia and fears Goneril's ingratitude is driving him mad.

## Analysis

### Lear isolated

This scene suggests Lear's growing isolation and fragile mental state. Lear is so distracted by disturbing thoughts that he hardly engages with the Fool. His recognition that he has mistreated Cordelia increases the sense of isolation. We suspect that Regan will receive him coldly. Soon Lear will have no one to turn to; he will be isolated from all his daughters.

**A02**

# Study focus: Lear in denial

Lear is blind to a number of truths. He does not recognise his faults as a father (in his view, his troubles are all caused by his ungrateful offspring), and we know he has little chance of regaining his earlier authority. It is only when his kingly mentality has been broken down by suffering that he will be able to perceive and understand the reality of his situation. After the tension and violent emotions of Act I Scene 5, the Fool's vulgar rhyme which closes the scene comes as a moment of light relief. An interval (however short) is welcome; we know that Lear's suffering has started in earnest.

# Key quotation: The role of the Fool

**A02**

When, despite his mental turmoil, Lear is able to answer one of the Fool's riddles, the Fool congratulates him **ironically**: 'thou would'st make a good Fool' (line 36).

The Fool has taken on the **paradoxical** task of distracting Lear from the immediate pain of his situation while making him face up to his responsibility for creating it in the first place. On this occasion the Fool succeeds in engaging Lear, but when Lear answers the riddle the Fool deprives him of triumph by telling him that his success is worthy only of a fool. To compare a king to a fool is clearly an insult, deflating for Lear and amusing for the audience, but it also raises the issue of the Fool's nature. A fool might be a professional entertainer or a natural eccentric. This fool seems to be a 'natural', but a perceptive one in the point he is making. To recover from being a bad king, Lear will indeed need the perspective of 'a good Fool' and to be prepared to humble himself.

# Revision task 1: Changing characters

**A02**

Make notes on which characters have changed in the first Act, and how. Write about:
- Changes in their position and status
- Changes in their personality

# ACT II SCENE 1

## Summary

- Cornwall and Regan are expected at Gloucester's house. Edmund determines to use their arrival to his own advantage. There is gossip concerning 'likely wars' (line 10) between Cornwall and Albany.

- Edmund calls Edgar down from his hiding place and tells him he must escape at once. He asks Edgar whether he has spoken against Cornwall, implying that Cornwall and Regan are as enraged against him as Gloucester. Edmund then draws Edgar into a mock fight.

- After Edgar flees, Edmund deliberately wounds himself and cries out for help. He claims that Edgar tried to involve him in a plan to murder Gloucester. Gloucester says that Edgar will be executed.

- Cornwall and Regan arrive. Gloucester praises Edmund as a 'Loyal and natural boy' (line 83) and says he will disinherit Edgar. Regan asks whether Edgar was egged on by Lear's riotous knights. She has received Goneril's letter. Like her, Regan has no intention of giving Lear's followers house room. (The real reason why she and Cornwall have come to visit Gloucester is to avoid receiving Lear and his men.)

- Edmund now promises to serve Cornwall.

## Analysis

### Edmund's success

In this scene we see the evil characters continue to gain ground. Edmund's plans prosper and he now aligns himself with Cornwall and Regan; **plot** and **subplot** become intertwined. Edmund's quick wits help him here. He is able to respond to events, as well as control them. His lines to Edgar at the start of the scene are full of short, sharp statements and questions, suggesting his command of circumstances. It is possible that Edmund intends to kill Edgar and claim self-defence but is thwarted by the fighting skills which Edgar displays later in the play. Whatever the case, Edmund achieves with terrifying ease the goal of dispossessing his brother which he set himself in Act I Scene 2, indicating how effortlessly evil begins to run riot in the kingdom. When Edmund offers his services to Cornwall we wonder what he is hoping to gain now.

**A03   KEY CONTEXT**

Edmund is **Machiavellian**, like other Shakespearean villains such as Iago and Richard III. Shakespeare's contemporaries misunderstood the works of the influential Florentine writer, Niccolo Machiavelli, believing he proposed that rulers should behave in immoral and corrupt ways. Edmund's Machiavellian practices include deception, betrayal and sexual misconduct.

**KEY CONTEXT**  **A03**

In Shakespeare's theatre it was not possible to dim the stage lighting to show that it was night time. Instead, darkness had to be conveyed to the audience by the comments of the characters ('Here stood he in the dark', line 37) and the presence of actors carrying flaming torches ('Torches! Torches!', line 32). It is **ironic** that Edmund calls for light so that everyone can see what is happening, when his real intention is to cover up the truth of what has taken place between himself and Edgar.

## Character development

One of this play's strengths is the way in which the main characters respond to the rapid unfolding of events by revealing new or hidden sides to themselves. Edmund becomes more openly selfish and evil as events grant him the opportunity, as do Goneril, Regan and Cornwall. Lear and Gloucester are complacent and unperceptive when they have authority, but respond to their fall with a mixture of disillusionment and integrity which turns them into far more sympathetic figures. Meanwhile Albany, having seen his wife Goneril for what she is, graduates from a rather ineffectual husband into a determined general. Finally, we will see Edgar grow from a bewildered fugitive into an epitome of patience, cunning and even ruthlessness.

## Progress booster: Character assessment

As the play moves between **plot** and **subplot**, we rejoin the characters at new stages in their development. Our assessment of the characters is therefore bound to change as the play progresses. You should be able to discuss how our knowledge of them is built up by their words and actions from scene to scene. At this stage, for example, the audience may well still side with Edmund against Gloucester and Edgar. After all, Edmund has been the underdog and his actions show his courage and ingenuity, as well as his opponents' gullibility.

**KEY INTERPRETATION**  **A05**

Unlike Gloucester, we know that Edgar is innocent and Edmund anything but a 'Loyal and natural boy' (line 83). We watch in frustration as Edmund deceives his father and forms an alliance with Cornwall and Regan, and we wait in suspense for the truth to come out. This use by Shakespeare of **dramatic irony** ensures the audience are fully engaged with the play. Can you find other examples of this device?

## Gloucester is vulnerable and isolated

Gloucester seems to be so unnerved by the supposed threat from Edgar (perhaps sensing his weakness before the rising generation) that he not only ignores Edmund's injuries but disowns Edgar without a second thought. His hasty reaction gives us the impression that he is self-centred and lacking in judgement. In his panic, Gloucester follows Edmund's lead entirely and appears to be overwhelmed. Like Lear, he seems vulnerable, as indicated by his speech to Regan ('my old heart is cracked, it's cracked', line 89). Gloucester is also isolated in this scene. As the evil characters draw closer together, he has little to say. Regan and Cornwall are as smooth and assured as Edmund. Both assume a commanding tone.

## Regan begins to show her true self

Regan's comforting and affectionate words to Gloucester are perhaps surprising. Shakespeare is leaving her true nature partially concealed, for maximum dramatic impact in Act II Scene 4. However, we are likely to distrust her; she and Goneril share the same low opinion of Lear's followers, and Regan has deliberately chosen to thwart her father's plans by coming to visit Gloucester. Essentially, she is denying her father shelter.

## Revision task 2: Loyalty and disloyalty  **A02**

Cornwall tells Edmund, 'you shall be ours' (line 113) and Edmund replies, 'I shall serve you, Sir' (line 115). Make notes on:

● Which characters owe allegiance to others
● Whether in your view they serve them loyally or let them down

# ACT II SCENE 2

## Summary

- Kent and Oswald meet outside Gloucester's house. Kent accuses Oswald of being a conceited coward (amongst other things). When Kent challenges him to a fight, Oswald runs from him, yelling out for help.

- Edmund tries to part the two men, but Kent is keen to punish Oswald. Cornwall stops the fight. When asked why he dislikes Oswald so much, Kent says his face offends him. He then insults Cornwall and the others.

- Kent is placed in the stocks as a punishment. He protests that he is on the king's business, and should not be treated in this degrading fashion. Gloucester agrees, but Cornwall sweeps his objections aside. Gloucester stays behind to offer his condolences to Kent. Kent is stoical and says he'll 'sleep out' (line 152) his time in the stocks.

- Alone on stage, Kent reveals that he has a letter from Cordelia. She intends to put right all the wrongs that have been done to Lear since she was banished.

## Analysis

### Bad servants

The audience will enjoy Kent's long list of imaginative and lively insults, and his slapstick chase of Oswald around the stage. Oswald is a worthy object of scorn and the quarrel at the start of the scene provides a moment of comic relief and entertaining action. Behind Kent's insults lies a serious point, however: the dangers of the bad servant. It is possible to argue that *King Lear* is full of bad servants, who subvert the order that they should be serving faithfully.

This list could include Goneril, Regan and Cornwall, but also Gloucester and even Lear himself. Each character has a responsibility to serve the British social order but fails to uphold the standard of justice needed to make it stable and effective, generally because they put themselves above the public good instead of following their duties. It may be argued in Oswald's defence that he always does what he's told by Regan, but does this make him a good servant? There is a strong contrast between the compliant Oswald and the outspoken Kent, who is so dedicated to Lear that he is prepared to tell him plainly when he is making a bad decision.

# Study focus: The loyal Kent

**A02**

Kent is a loyal servant to Lear. In Act I Scene 1, he bravely tries to make Lear see the foolishness of his actions. Later, in Act I Scene 4 and Act II Scene 2, Kent attacks Oswald for working against Lear, then shows his contempt for the authority of Cornwall and Regan. However, Kent's actions and blunt speech consistently fail to improve Lear's prospects and arguably make his situation worse each time.

Should we conclude that Kent's behaviour is misguided? Perhaps he is deliberately seeking confrontation, as it is the only way available to him to bring the issues out into the open?

**KEY CONTEXT** **A03**

The stocks was a device of wooden boards which locked around the victim's ankles (and sometimes the wrists), leaving him or her trapped in an uncomfortable, publicly humiliating position, exposed to all weathers as well as to the abuse of passers-by. In Shakespeare's day it seems to have been considered a particularly suitable form of punishment for servants who had misbehaved. For a former Earl of Kent, this would be a particularly demeaning punishment.

## Appearance and reality

Kent makes a serious point when he says he does not like the faces he sees before him; unlike Lear, he is not fooled by appearances and recognises Cornwall, Regan and Oswald for what they are. He voices the concerns of the audience when he insults Cornwall. However, Kent is punished again for his goodness and honesty, as Cordelia and Edgar have been punished in spite of their virtues.

## Cornwall and Regan in control

The punishment of Kent is significant for other reasons. We see that Cornwall is arrogant, snapping, 'I'll answer that' when Gloucester fears he will offend Lear (line 143), and we see that Regan is vindictive, urging that Kent's time in the stocks be greatly lengthened. It becomes clear that husband and wife operate effectively as a team and enjoy their cruelty, hinting at the horrors to come in Act III Scene 7.

It is also clear that power is in new hands. Gloucester is ineffectual in this scene, and Lear's representative, Kent, is treated with scorn. Only the hint that Cordelia will return offers us some hope that the progress of the evil characters might be checked.

## Key quotation: The wheel of Fortune

**A02**

Kent closes the scene by addressing the 'goddess' Fortune: 'Fortune, good night; smile once more; turn thy wheel!' (line 169).

Fortune was traditionally visualised as a wheel that carries people up to prosperity and down to adversity. Since people had limited control over their fate, the best course in bad times was to be patient and simply wait for a turn of the wheel, as Kent does here. Throughout the play, characters manage the rise and fall of their fortunes with varying degrees of success, sometimes misunderstanding their position as Edgar does at IV.1.3, sometimes seeing it all too clearly as Edmund does at V.3.174.

# ACT II SCENE 3

## Summary

- Edgar has heard himself proclaimed a criminal and has concealed himself in a tree. His position is desperate; he cannot attempt to flee England as all the ports (seaports and town gates) are watched and his father's men roam the countryside trying to hunt him down.

- To preserve his life Edgar decides to disguise himself as a 'Bedlam beggar' (line 14). He describes what he will do to effect this disguise: knot his hair, cover himself in dirt, stick sharp objects in his arms, and wear only a blanket for protection.

## Analysis

### Edgar in desperation

Edgar's **soliloquy** leaves the audience in no doubt as to the difficulties he will face. The fact that he chooses to disguise himself as a social outcast reveals his desperation and the danger he is in. In Shakespeare's day 'Bedlam' (Bethlehem) hospital housed the mentally ill. When they were released, Bedlam inmates were allowed to go begging for survival; this is what Edgar has been reduced to by his brother and father. As in the previous scene, we see goodness pushed aside, degraded and punished.

While Edgar speaks at the front of the stage, the audience can still see Kent sleeping in the stocks behind him. This juxtaposition creates a visual comparison between the two men, both of whom have to disguise themselves in humiliating ways while the evil prosper. Edgar's situation also mirrors Lear's. Edgar is now reliant on charity, his world and expectations turned upside down. We get a glimpse of what Lear will be reduced to. Edgar's assumed 'madness' also points towards what will happen to Lear in Act III.

**A02**

# Study focus: Edgar becomes cunning

Despite Edgar's degradation, it is possible to see something positive in this brief scene. So far Edgar has been easily manipulated by Edmund, who calls him 'a brother noble, / Whose nature is so far from doing harms / That he suspects none' (I.2.183–5). However, with his survival at stake, Edgar shows a new side to his character. Just as we saw Edmund cutting himself with a sword in Act II Scene 1 in order to fool Gloucester into believing he had been hurt by Edmund, now we see Edgar self-harming in order to fool his pursuers into believing he is a mentally-disturbed outcast. Has Edgar already matched his brother in cunning?

## Key quotation: Poor Tom    **A02**

Edgar puts his faith in his new guise as Poor Tom and proclaims, 'Edgar I nothing am' (line 21). 'Am' probably rhymes with 'Tom' as Edgar slips into a rural accent to conceal his voice.

The word 'nothing' chimes through the play, as characters are forced to abandon their normal lives and identities, driven ever closer towards breakdown and death. But is Edgar right that he is losing his true self, or does his role as Tom have the potential to equip him with greater understanding, flexibility and opportunity?

**A03** **KEY CONTEXT**

The theatrical convention of the impenetrable disguise was frequently used in Jacobean drama. Audiences accepted that characters would not recognise someone in disguise. There are many examples of important characters who adopt a disguise in Shakespeare's plays; for example, in *Measure for Measure*, Duke Vincentio pretends to be a friar so that he can spy on his people. In *King Lear*, Edgar and Kent are forced to conceal their identities to preserve their lives.

# ACT II SCENE 4

## Summary

- Lear arrives at Gloucester's house. He refuses to believe that Cornwall and Regan are responsible for Kent's 'shame' in the stocks (line 6).

- Regan and Cornwall send word that they are sick and weary and cannot speak with him. When Gloucester tries to excuse Cornwall's behaviour, Lear is enraged. He feels himself becoming hysterical and tries to control himself.

- Cornwall and Regan arrive. Regan tells her father that he should accept his age and failing powers of judgement and be led by others. When Lear complains about Goneril, Regan snaps back that he will curse her too 'When the rash mood is on' (line 168). Cornwall admits he was responsible for Kent's punishment.

- When Goneril arrives, Lear curses her and considers staying with Regan, but Regan too suggests a reduction in his train of followers. Lear tries to remind his daughters that he gave them everything. They are not impressed. Gradually they argue Lear out of all of his knights.

- Lear threatens his daughters that he will be revenged on them. As the storm starts he angrily refuses to weep but cries out, 'O Fool! I shall go mad' (line 285) and rushes out.

- Gloucester is concerned about Lear's well-being; the countryside he has gone out into offers very little protection from the elements. But his 'guests' insist that Lear should be left to suffer the consequences of his actions. Regan instructs Gloucester to lock the doors, maintaining that the king's followers are dangerous. Lear is left outside in the storm.

## KEY CONTEXT

Rich householders and European rulers had employed fools as entertainers for many generations. There were female as well as male fools. Fools wore distinctive dress and were multi-talented individuals; they sang, danced, performed acrobatics and told jokes and riddles. Some, like Lear's fool, were expected to be wittily critical of their masters and guests, though if they went too far they risked a whipping.

## Analysis

### Lear's powerlessness

This scene presents Lear with a number of difficulties which he finds insurmountable. We watch anxiously as his power and self-possession are stripped away through the course of the scene. A number of events and speeches early in the scene point towards the stark outcome, when Lear is rejected by his elder daughters. Kent's presence in the stocks unnerves the king; it is proof that he continues to be treated with contempt, a point reinforced by Cornwall and Regan's refusal to speak with him. Revealingly, Lear seeks Regan out himself instead of sending a servant to fetch her. He is now reduced to conveying his own messages.

His powerlessness is emphasised again when his requests for information are ignored; he asks many times how Kent came to be in the stocks before receiving an answer. Lear's changes of mood and tone indicate his increasing mental instability. The Fool's disturbing little tales of misguided kindness also operate as a choric introduction (see **chorus**) to the 'cruel kindness' that Goneril and Regan display later in the scene. The perfunctory and frosty greeting between Lear, Cornwall and Regan suggests that Lear is foolish to pin his hopes on his second daughter's kindness. His belief that she would never 'oppose the bolt / Against my coming in' (lines 175–6) is chillingly misplaced.

### The daughters triumph

Goneril's entrance proves to be the turning point for the beleaguered king. Her lack of concern about whether Lear returns to her or not proves that the sisters are indifferent to their father's agitation and suffering. Goneril and Regan are extremely firm and authoritative when 'measuring out' Lear's knights for him. We are reminded of the dangers of measuring love in words and numbers. Lear's insistence that he will stay with the daughter who allows him to retain the greatest number of followers is as blind and foolish as his love-test in Act I Scene 1. Can he not see that neither of his daughters cares for him? His bargaining is desperate, as impotent as his curses and threats of revenge. He rushes out into the storm.

**A03** **KEY CONTEXT**

Renaissance medical theory was based on ideas that were arrived at during the Middle Ages. Shakespeare's contemporaries believed in substances in the body called the four 'humours'. The imbalance of these produced different types of personality. Lear is a choleric man (with too much fire in his system, hence short-tempered and rash), a disposition which might be considered one of the causes of his mental ill health.

## Study focus: The daughters in control **A02**

The tone of the speeches that follow Lear's exit is very telling. Goneril, Regan and Cornwall are unmoved by Lear's agonised final speech; their cool control contrasts starkly with his wild passion. There is a cruel desire to inflict punishment on 'the old man' (line 287) – more contemptuous words. By now the audience will recognise the hypocrisy of Regan's fears about Lear's knights.

This scene has proved that Goneril and Regan are expert manipulators, ready to use any excuse to justify their own actions. When the storm starts, we know that they have 'won'. Lear's fear about his own mind, first voiced in Act I Scene 4, has been realised.

## Progress booster: Gendered characteristics **A02**

When Lear feels a surge of emotion that leaves him stunned and giddy, he describes it as 'this mother' and calls it also by its medical name, 'hysterica passio' (lines 54–5). This was a form of hysteria that could affect either men or women, but which was originally supposed by doctors to be a female condition originating in the womb. Lear's use of the two terms suggests that he regards his emotional state as a female weakness, undermining his masculine strength. He has a similar reaction at line 276 when he feels himself close to crying and condemns his tears as mere 'women's weapons'.

Some critics see these references as part of a network of gendered characteristics in the play – father/daughter bonds, the absent Mrs Lear, Lear's own misogyny – in which the feminine is routinely suppressed or denigrated. Can you find other specific examples of hostility to female qualities in the play?

## Key quotation: Human needs **A02**

Lear explains, 'Allow not nature more than nature needs, / Man's life is cheap as beast's' (lines 265–6). He means that human beings need more than just the basics for staying alive; they need self-esteem, the regard of others, valued possessions and so on. Lear speaks from the heart and, suddenly stripped of such supports, he breaks down.

# EXTRACT ANALYSIS: II.4.216–85

This extract is a turning point for Lear. Despite the Fool's comments, he has managed to remain in denial about the damage he has done to himself and his country. Now the truth is becoming impossible to ignore. Not only has Kent been found in the stocks, but Lear's questions about his servant's punishment have also been disregarded. He has been treated insolently by Regan and Cornwall, his authority challenged. By the time Goneril arrives, Lear has become an increasingly impotent figure.

We know that Lear can expect further trouble when Regan greets Goneril warmly. The sisters are united and ready to strike. The subject of Lear's followers proves to be his undoing, as we suspected it might be when Goneril complained about them in Act I Scene 4. To the beleaguered king his followers represent himself: his status, dignity, authority. In other words, they represent Lear as he was. By reducing their number, Goneril and Regan show their father that he no longer has a role to play: he is nothing.

Goneril and Regan's reduction of Lear's followers is a masterpiece of orchestrated cruelty. The sisters use a variety of hypocritical excuses to dismiss Lear's men. Regan tells Lear that 'both charge and danger / Speak 'gainst so great a number' (lines 238–9). It would be impossible for 'two commands' in one household to 'Hold amity'. She adds that if Lear had fewer followers, they would be easier to command (but note who is to do the commanding – the new royal 'we' – Goneril and Regan). Finally, Goneril suggests that Lear needs no one to attend him since she already has plenty of servants to do the job. Here we see Goneril and Regan at their most brutally efficient. Not a word is wasted.

Impatient to get their work done, the sisters cut Lear off when he is speaking. At the end of their swift 'discussion', Regan finishes her elder sister's train of thought with a stark, short question. Their tone has been hectoring and authoritarian throughout. Regan is particularly vicious. Her 'And in good time you gave it' (line 249) is as mean-spirited and chilling as her brazen question, 'What need one?' (line 262). Regan's role as 'leader' in this scene ensures that Lear's annihilation is merciless. During Act I Scene 4 we realised Goneril was ferocious. Now the other daughter proves herself to be every bit as callous.

At first, Lear cannot quite believe what is happening. He struggles to maintain his dignity. His opening lines to Goneril show his desperation: 'I prithee, daughter, do not make me mad: / I will not trouble thee my child; farewell' (lines 217–8). His politeness is pitiful. Two lines later Lear is angry again. He calls Goneril 'a disease that's in my flesh, … a boil, / A plague-sore, or embossed carbuncle' (lines 221–3). The **imagery** of disease is apt. It accompanies the images of predatory animals used to describe Goneril and Regan and emphasises how Lear is being assaulted by his own flesh and blood. These images are followed by thoughts of vengeance, although Lear again tries to be patient:

… But I'll not chide thee;
Let shame come when it will, I do not call it;
I do not bid the thunder-bearer shoot,
Nor tell tales of thee to high-judging Jove. (lines 224–7)

Lear hopes – understandably – that the gods will punish his ungrateful daughter. However, his insistence that he will not 'tell tales' seems childish. And his tolerance is revealed as blindness when he says 'I can be patient; I can stay with Regan, / I and my hundred knights' (lines 229–30). How little Lear has learned. He cannot shake off the idea that love is a commodity that can be bought, pleading, 'I gave you all' (line 249).

Like Edgar in the previous scene, Lear is reduced to a state of beggary, reliant on a hostile world for charity. He begins to speak like the helpless dependant he is:

You Heavens, give me that patience, patience I need! –
You see me here, you Gods, a poor old man,
As full of grief as age; wretched in both!
If it be you that stirs these daughters' hearts
Against their father, fool me not so much
To bear it tamely (lines 270–5)

Lear is overwhelmed by wretchedness, terrified that his 'daughters' hearts' (line 273) will defeat him. In this speech Lear also starts to consider what a man is, what true necessity means, ideas that will preoccupy him in Act III. But how much truth does Lear really face? His description of himself may be accurate, but he is full of self-pity, moving very quickly from considering what man needs, to his own 'true need' (line 269). He sees only the sins of others. Some see Lear's request to be touched by 'noble anger' (line 275) and his furious refusal to weep as signs that he is still blindly clinging to his regal persona. However, it is impossible not to pity Lear here. His struggle not to bear cruel treatment 'tamely' is impressive (line 275). This stoicism may not restore his power, but Lear's pride and fortitude can be seen as the qualities of a true tragic hero.

Lear's last speech shows the mixture of courage and fear he has displayed throughout the scene. His incomplete threats (lines 278–81) are signs that he no longer has any control over his daughters, or his mind. Although he is reduced to bluster, his desire for vengeance will still strike a chord with the audience: Goneril and Regan deserve to be punished. Our sympathy increases with Lear's dramatic and agonised exit, 'O Fool! I shall go mad' (line 285). The stage direction (*Storm heard at a distance*) also provides an ominous warning of the suffering to come.

In this extract there has been an unrelenting march towards a vicious new world, where only the fittest will survive. Regardless of the reservations we may feel about Lear and his actions, we appreciate the **pathos** of the king's situation. He has been forced to confront the truth about his daughters in a very cruel way. This extract shows Goneril and Regan ruthlessly in control, their energy undiminished. What new atrocities can we expect from them in Act III?

**A03** **KEY CONTEXT**

For a king to be treated as Lear is, would surely have shocked the original audience. James I, who saw the play acted in 1606, had strong convictions about the divine right of kings. This meant he believed that, as king, he had a God-given right to rule the country and was untouchable. In 1610 he told parliament, 'Kings are not only God's lieutenants upon earth, and sit upon God's throne, but even by God himself they are called gods.'

# ACT III SCENE 1

## Summary

- Out on the heath, Kent is searching for Lear. Kent meets a Gentleman, one of Lear's knights, and asks him where Lear has gone.
- We learn that the king is out in the open, raging against the elements. The Fool is his only companion; he is trying to distract his master with jokes. The Gentleman paints a vivid picture of Lear, tearing his hair, running about unprotected, calling for the destruction of the world.
- Kent speaks of the recent 'division' or rivalry between Albany and Cornwall. He goes on to explain that the King of France is preparing to invade England, having already sent some of his army across secretly, accompanied by Cordelia.
- Kent gives the Gentleman a ring and asks him to deliver it to Cordelia. They continue searching for Lear.

## Analysis

### A world of suffering

Act III occurs in short scenes to allow us to see Lear's swift and dramatic descent from rationality. We also learn what happens to Lear's mirror image, Gloucester. There is a spiralling downwards for both characters, culminating in a scene of appalling violence against Gloucester. Lear and Gloucester become heroic, tragic figures in Act III, their two stories developing side by side to reinforce our sense of a world torn apart by suffering.

The Gentleman's descriptions of Lear on the heath prepare us for the sight of the king in the next scene. He is hatless ('unbonneted'), showing a loss of royal dignity, and is behaving irrationally, shouting at the storm and tearing his hair. The description also establishes the violence of the storm, which **symbolises** the destructive power Lear has unleashed across his family and nation, as well as on himself.

## Progress booster: Correspondences

There was a widespread notion, dating back to medieval times, that there was a correspondence between how nature was ordered on Earth and in the heavens. At times of crisis, significant events in the world of individuals (the microcosm) might be mirrored in the natural world (the macrocosm). In *Macbeth*, for example, the murder of King Duncan triggers a storm, an earthquake and unnatural behaviour by animals. Shakespeare draws upon this idea when Lear's division of his kingdom is mirrored in an immense breakdown of the weather. We see it also in the simultaneous breakdown of his family, Gloucester's family and his own mind.

Be aware of how **tragedy** spreads throughout the play through such correspondences and be prepared to comment on their dramatic effect.

# ACT III SCENE 2

## Summary

- Increasingly erratic, Lear rants in the storm. He ignores the Fool when he pleads with him to return to Gloucester's house to ask for shelter.
- Kent arrives and spies a hovel nearby. He tries to persuade Lear to take shelter there. He intends to return to Gloucester's house and beg Goneril and Regan to take their father in.
- We see a new side of Lear's character when he expresses concern for the Fool and identifies with his suffering. Now he recognises how precious such things as shelter are. Lear asks Kent to lead them to the hovel.
- Left alone on stage, the Fool makes predictions about Albion's (Britain's) future and speaks whimsically of a utopia where evil will cease to exist.

## Analysis

### Study focus: The storm **(A02)**

Note that Lear's speeches establish and reflect the properties of the storm. They are full of anger and distress, as he moves swiftly from one topic to another. The violence of the **imagery** Lear employs reflects his state of mind. Lear's isolation is shown by his lack of interaction with the other characters on stage, which also indicates that he is now engaged in an internal struggle; he is battling to preserve his wits. The storm serves as a **metaphor** for Lear's – and Britain's – plight. Lear's obsession with justice and criminal behaviour, introduced in this scene, is maintained until the end of the play. Suffering has made the king start to consider issues he took too little care of as ruler; his journey towards greater understanding of himself and the world around him has begun.

### The Fool's prophecy

There are two ways of interpreting the Fool's prophecy. The Fool is either suggesting – optimistically – that virtue will triumph in England, or sarcastically suggesting that optimism about the future would be misplaced; even in these terrible days men use their feet for walking. The Fool again provides a moment of relief, a pause in the action where the audience can gather their thoughts.

## Key quotation: To what extent is Lear changing? **(A02)**

Lear claims he is 'a man / More sinned against than sinning' (lines 59–60).

After a lifetime in charge, the experience of being stripped of authority and thrown out into the storm begins to make Lear realise what life is like for people who have no power. At this stage, however, he is not ready to face up to his own failings as a king and a father. Instead, he thinks how others deserve punishment, calling himself a victim more than a wrongdoer.

**(A03) KEY CONTEXT**

On the Renaissance stage, the sound of thunder was created in one of two ways, either by rolling an iron ball on a sheet of metal, or by beating a drum. Lightning could be simulated by the use of fireworks.

**(A04) KEY CONNECTION**

In medieval literature there was a tradition of moral criticism of the rich for their callous treatment of the poor. Lear's criticism of the justice system fits into this tradition. During the same period that *King Lear* was written, Shakespeare also wrote *Measure for Measure*, which questions many ideas about authority and justice.

# EXTRACT ANALYSIS: III.2.1–73

Lear's elder daughters have stripped him of his power and status, abandoning him to the dreadful storm. As his mind breaks down, he begins to see reality in a new light and to confront unpleasant truths. The style and structure of Lear's speeches convey the king's confused, violent state of mind. We see anger, a desire for revenge, egotism and, more positively, humility and a recognition of previous mistakes.

Lear's speeches also reflect the movements of the storm. Lear's opening line, 'Blow, winds … rage! blow!' (line 1) is like a crack of thunder, suggesting that Shakespeare is using Lear's language to create the effects of the storm for the audience. Lear *is* the storm. His actions have led to misrule in the kingdom, and nature reflects that chaos. Lear has made others suffer, now the storm makes him suffer.

Lear wants to see the world destroyed by 'cataracts and hurricanoes' (line 2) because of the treachery of 'ingrateful man' (line 9). These last two words indicate that Lear blames Goneril and Regan for his suffering. But he also seems to welcome his own destruction when he yells, 'Singe my white head!' (line 6). Perhaps this is an acknowledgement of his sins, a desire to be punished. Nonetheless, Lear continues to act out the role of mighty monarch. His first speech is a long list of commands. He expects the tempest to do his bidding. Has Lear really woken up to his errors?

Lear's second speech is less explosive, but still full of rage:

I tax not you, you elements, with unkindness;
I never gave you kingdom, called you children.
You owe me no subscription: then let fall
Your horrible pleasure. (lines 16–9)

Now Lear recognises that he cannot rule the elements. He says – with crazy egotism – that they owe him no loyalty. These lines continue the theme of 'ingrateful man' (line 9) and sum up the lunatic king's version of events so far. Lear's words convey the self-pity he feels: 'here I stand, your slave, / A poor, infirm, weak, and despised old man' (lines 19–20). This description might be seen as the accurate self-assessment of a man who is beginning to see himself more clearly. Lear's reference to himself as a slave is significant. In Act II Scene 4 he said he would rather work as Oswald's slave than return to Goneril. Now he begins to see that he has – indeed is – nothing. His paranoid delusion that the storm is in league with his 'pernicious daughters' (line 22) seems to confirm his arrogant vulnerability.

The violence of the storm and his daughters' treachery push Lear into considering criminals who remain 'Unwhipped of Justice' (line 53). He starts to look through new eyes at the lives of those he was responsible for as ruler, struggling to understand the world that has been revealed to him. However, Lear returns to himself again in the final lines of this speech: 'I am a man / More sinned against than sinning' (lines 59–60). This statement needs careful consideration. Is it true? Given the events of the final moments of the play, the judgement may yet go in Lear's favour.

While Lear welcomes the storm, Kent and the Fool show us how dreadful its effects are and guide our responses to Lear. Kent is aghast when he finds his master 'bare-headed' (line 60). The fact that Lear runs about 'unbonneted' (III.1.14) shows how far he has fallen since the start of Act I, when he had his crown and all the other trappings of majesty to protect him. Now Lear is mentally and physically exposed.

Kent's speech at lines 42–9 serves two purposes. His descriptions of the storm, with its 'sheets of fire', 'horrid thunder' and 'groans of roaring wind and rain' bring the tempest more vividly to life for the audience and reinforce its dangers. We are told that 'man's nature cannot carry / Th'affliction nor the fear' of such nights (lines 48–9). The Fool, who finds the storm very hard to bear, urges Lear to return and 'ask thy daughters blessing' (line 12). For the Fool to ask Lear to submit to his daughters, things must indeed be desperate on the heath. This desperation is forced home when Kent seems to suggest the same course of action at line 63.

The Fool's vulnerability also heightens and reflects Lear's. He shows us an attractive side of Lear's character. The king now finds time to feel for another: 'Come on, my boy. How dost, my boy? Art cold? … Poor fool and knave, I have one part in my heart / That's sorry yet for thee' (lines 68–73). These lines will impress the audience, although Lear is still obviously caught up in his own sufferings (only 'one part' of his heart feels sorry for the Fool). But who can blame Lear for focusing on his own agony here? It is clear that he is increasingly isolated. He hardly acknowledges his companions on the heath until he speaks to the Fool at line 68.

This scene is significant for several reasons. It shows us Lear in the first stages of his mental breakdown and we see the outcome we expected at the end of Act II Scene 4. We learn that Lear is preoccupied by thoughts about filial ingratitude but also considers broader questions as he struggles to retain his wits. We see him start to move towards greater self-awareness and, in spite of his continued egotism, Lear becomes more generous.

The storm reflects the terrible state England is now in, ruled by cruel monsters. The hostile setting and violent **imagery** increase our fears about events to come and make us fear for Lear's safety. How will the king survive this night, which seems so unendurable? The scene also offers us a faint glimmer of hope about human nature. The Fool and Kent stick by their master, the Fool calling Lear by the affectionate name 'nuncle' and Kent insisting on addressing Lear respectfully as 'my lord'. These flashes of compassion are vital in Act III, which closes with an act of appalling inhumanity.

**A03  KEY CONTEXT**

Since the late eighteenth century, productions have often gone out of their way to unleash impressive storm effects. Trevor Nunn's 1976 production and Kenneth Branagh's 1991 production, for example, featured simulated rain on stage. However, because Lear's voice needs to be audible to the audience above the storm, this type of realism has sometimes been counter-productive, leaving the actor shouting unintelligibly over a cacophony of thunder and wind effects.

........................................................

# ACT III SCENE 3

........................................

## Summary

........................................

- Gloucester frets about the 'unnatural dealing' (lines 1–2) of Cornwall, Regan and Goneril, who have warned him against helping Lear.
- He tells Edmund that Albany and Cornwall are set to clash and that the King of France has begun his invasion to restore Lear.
- When Gloucester leaves to find the king, Edmund announces his intention to betray his father to Cornwall.

........................................

## Analysis

........................................

## Study focus: Gloucester in danger

This scene is full of important revelations. Our impression that Cornwall, Goneril and Regan are ruthless bullies is confirmed when Gloucester tells Edmund that they have now taken control of his house and forbidden him even to speak about Lear. Edmund's exclamation, 'Most savage and unnatural!' (line 7) assures Gloucester that his son shares his feelings of disgust about this, but the audience hears Edmund's sarcasm all too clearly. When Gloucester reveals that he has received a 'dangerous' letter (line 10) concerning military support for the king, we at once realise that he has put himself in dreadful danger. If Edmund tells the sisters about the letter, they will condemn Gloucester as a traitor.

### Edmund's ruthlessness

Edmund now has his sights set on his father's title. His decision to betray him is made without a moment's hesitation, befitting Edmund's ruthless nature. In contrast, Gloucester has prevaricated and shows here that he is anxious about his decision to support Lear. Gloucester's feverish fretting mirrors the alarm the audience will feel at the end of this scene; we are sure Gloucester is in great danger now. Evil continues to triumph, and good intentions will again be thwarted. Gloucester's earnest desire to assist Lear seems as hopeless and doomed as Kent and the Fool's concern in the previous scene.

Edmund's final line in the scene – 'The younger rises when the old doth fall' (line 25) – stresses inter-generational rivalry as a key motivator of the play. In early modern England the older generation held power and authority over the young. Some members of the audience would probably have sympathised with Edmund's desire to get power for himself, if not necessarily with the methods he employs.

## Key quotation: Understanding Gloucester's character   **A02**

Gloucester tells Edmund, 'If I die for it, as no less is threatened me, the King, my old master, must be relieved' (lines 17–9; by 'relieved' he means rescued).

It is chillingly clear how far Goneril, Regan and Cornwall have taken control, not only seizing Gloucester's house but threatening him with death if he offers the king any help. Until now we have seen Gloucester as a rather ineffectual figure, easily swayed by others, but in this moment of crisis his integrity becomes apparent. As is also the case with Lear and Edgar, the **tragic** situation in which he finds himself presents him with a challenge to which he rises, in so doing achieving a degree of greatness which he had not shown before.

# ACT III SCENE 4

## Summary

- Kent urges Lear to take shelter in the hovel, but the storm is less distressing to Lear than his inner torment.
- The Fool rushes out of the hovel, scared by a creature he has found there. The 'spirit' (line 39) proves to be Edgar disguised as Poor Tom.
- Lear recognises his own misery in Tom, who describes his life hounded by the 'foul fiend' (line 45). Edgar has invented this account of a servant who, driven by lechery, has lost his income, deteriorated mentally and been reduced to begging.
- Lear has begun to feel empathy for the dispossessed and believes that he sees humanity in its essence when he looks at Tom. Lear decides that man is really 'a poor, bare, forked animal' (line 110). He tries to undress, to remove the superficial trappings that stand between him and 'unaccommodated man' (line 109). Kent and the Fool try to prevent him.
- During the confusion, Gloucester appears. He is dismayed to see the king in such poor company and urges Lear to go with him to a safe place. Despite the pleas of Gloucester and Kent, Lear continues to be most concerned for Poor Tom.
- Gloucester tells Kent that Goneril and Regan seek Lear's death. He also speaks of his own suffering; thoughts of his son's betrayal have sent him wild with grief. When Gloucester tells Tom to go into the hovel, Lear adds 'Come, let's in all' (line 176). Kent finally accepts Tom and the characters enter the hovel.

## Analysis

### Isolation

This is a scene of isolation and suffering. Each character is oppressed by his own concerns. Kent is agitated because Lear suffers; the Fool shivers in the storm. Both are helpless bystanders. Like Lear, Gloucester is preoccupied by thoughts of filial ingratitude. Edgar's breathless craziness is not only a way of disguising himself, but reflects his own sufferings as an outcast. His speeches are erratic in a way that Lear's are not, full of terrifying descriptions of physical and mental violence.

### Lear learns pity

Lear's concern for Kent, the Fool and Poor Tom suggests that he is learning compassion, reflected in his lines about the fate of the homeless: 'O, I have ta'en / Too little care of this' (lines 32–3). He declares that the rich and powerful should experience what 'wretches' feel (line 34), as he is now doing, so that they will be motivated to give the poor their excess wealth. The pity we feel for Lear increases as he learns to pity others. We also realise that Lear has recognised the need to look beyond appearances when he tries to remove his clothing in order to become 'the thing itself' (lines 108–9), a human being without any status or pretensions.

---

**A03** **KEY CONTEXT**

Edgar's tales about the 'foul fiend' biting his back and tormenting him reflect Renaissance religious beliefs. People thought of the devil as a palpable presence, who walked about the world trying to tempt them into evil doing. The devil was also held responsible for ailments in people and animals, such as cataracts in the eye ('the web and the pin', lines 117–8).

**A03** **KEY CONTEXT**

'Flibberdigibbet' (line 116) is the name of a dancing devil. The names of many of the demons that appear in Act III, and some of the other language that Edgar uses as Poor Tom, were taken by Shakespeare from the book *A Declaration of Egregious Popish Impostures* by Samuel Harsnet, which appeared in 1603. In this book Harsnet, who was chaplain to the Bishop of London, wrote scathingly about fraudulent exorcisms carried out by Catholic priests. Edgar's language as Poor Tom reflects the language used by the victims of these exorcisms in Harsnet's book.

### KEY CONTEXT **A03**

Some critics have argued that Poor Tom's speeches contain critical comments about the legitimacy of the witchcraft trials that were held in England during the Elizabethan and Jacobean eras. Tom's 'madness' and history of evil-doing as a servant are a sham, while the real criminals, Goneril and Regan, cause devastation.

### PROGRESS BOOSTER **A05**

The settings in the play help to convey a sense of disorder, and the hovel is the ultimate expression of this. Later settings of chaos include the battlefield, the heath and Dover cliff. These settings are also linked to acts of violence: war, the storm, attempted suicide. Make sure you can write about the role played by different settings throughout the play.

## Edgar speaks of sin

Edgar's description of his life as a corrupt servant can be read as a comment on Oswald's career. Other commentators see Tom's story as a reminder of the seven deadly sins. His account of seven years as a beggar seems to be directed at his father, whom he will later judge harshly for his adultery in Act V Scene 3. Lear and Gloucester are both forced to face up to their sins in *King Lear*; Lear has already started to confront his failings.

### Study focus: Is Lear's view of human nature accurate? **A02**

Critics such as Jan Kott (see **page 24**) accept Lear's interpretation of Poor Tom as 'a poor, bare, forked animal' (line 110) and conclude that Shakespeare is giving us a wholly bleak picture of human existence, anticipating the twentieth-century literature of the **absurd.** Lear is mistaken, however, for Tom is actually Edgar, a highly purposeful, intelligent human being, acting the part of Tom in order to ensure his survival and ready to reclaim his rightful role if only he can find the opportunity.

In spite of the suffering displayed in this scene, some hope remains. It is also a positive element of the scene that the characters sympathise with one another, even though Kent is initially reluctant to allow Poor Tom to take shelter with the king. What is your view of the tone of the play at this point?

## A sombre mood

Overall, the prevailing mood is a sombre one. Poor Tom's references to the 'dark tower' (line 183) and the Jack the giant killer story in the final lines of the scene are ominous. Gloucester's house now holds four murderous predators (Goneril, Regan, Cornwall, Edmund) who are plotting against the two fathers.

## Revision task 3: The wisdom of fools **A02**

It is common in Shakespeare's plays for the greatest wisdom to come from characters who seem very foolish. Kent points out to Lear that his Fool's songs and jokes contain many perceptive comments: 'This is not altogether Fool, my Lord' (I.4.149). Sometimes an extreme state of mind or unorthodox point of view allows the characters to realise truths that others prefer not to notice.

Find examples of characters in the play whom others might class as mad or disturbed and note what truths they are able to express as a result of their unusual point of view.

# ACT III SCENE 5

## Summary

- Cornwall has been given the letter which contains information about the French invasion. He intends to punish Gloucester for his treachery.
- He sends Edmund to find his father. He also tells him that he is to be the new Earl of Gloucester, probably implying that his father will be executed.
- Edmund pretends to be torn between being loyal to Cornwall and faithful to his 'blood' (line 22), but secretly hopes that he will find his father with Lear. This will make Cornwall even more angry.

## Analysis

**A02**

### Study focus: Edmund's language

It is important that you can analyse characters' language closely. The first line of the scene ('I will have my revenge') suggests that violence is imminent. This is confirmed by Cornwall's consistently decisive and ruthless tone. Showing his customary facility with language, Edmund speaks politely and formally to Cornwall, who now acts as if he is the father of the nation. Edmund's exclamations in his second speech are emptily melodramatic, drawing attention to his chilling hypocrisy. Then in contrast, Edmund's aside to the audience a few seconds later is as vicious and cold blooded as his new patron's lines.

In earlier scenes we may have felt some admiration for Edmund as a spirited underdog, but here his sanctimonious willingness to hand over his own father to the merciless Cornwall shows him to be an out and out, despicable villain. Both of these evil men lust selfishly and destructively for power.

**A05** KEY INTERPRETATION

There are thirty-three references to letters during the course of the play. It has been argued that these not only contribute to the **plot** but add to the range of ideas and meaning depicted. Which letters in the play do you think have the most significance?

**A03** KEY CONTEXT

In the play as printed in 1608, and again in 1623, Edmund is routinely called 'Bastard' in speech prefixes and stage directions, perhaps stressing stock associations of the word with unpleasantness and impurity.

# ACT III SCENE 6

## Summary

- Lear conducts an imaginary trial of Goneril and Regan; Poor Tom mutters about the devil; the Fool continues to taunt Lear with home truths.
- Edgar is in tears as he listens to Lear's agony. His 'act' momentarily breaks down at 'Bless thy five wits!' (line 57). Kent implores Lear to be patient.
- Gloucester has gone for provisions, but he returns saying that Lear must be removed to safety because there is a plot to kill him. He has prepared a litter (a coach) to transport him to Dover, where he will be met by friends (the French forces).
- Kent is sorry that Lear must be disturbed, as he thinks sleep might have helped him regain his sanity.
- Left alone, Edgar reflects that his own problems seem lessened now that he has seen how much Lear is suffering. He expresses some hope for the future.

## Analysis

### Study focus: The mock trial

Notice how the cold-blooded discussion between Edmund and Cornwall in Act III Scene 5 contrasts sharply with the solicitous way Gloucester and Kent continue to behave towards Lear in Scene 6. Gloucester has found Lear a better shelter than the hovel, perhaps an outhouse or annex to his home. Lear's mock trial of Goneril and Regan is a parody of the love-test in Act I Scene 1. Here, however, Lear's judgement is not faulty. His 'madness' has helped him to see his daughters clearly.

While the Fool tries to dispel Lear's fantasies, pointing out that his comments on Goneril are actually being addressed to a stool, Edgar decides it will be more helpful to join in with the king, pretending to drive away the dogs that Lear imagines are barking at him. Edgar is so overcome by Lear's state that he begins to weep and is only just able to keep up his role as Poor Tom.

### The end of the Fool

The Fool speaks his last line in the play, 'And I'll go to bed at noon' (line 84). This comical remark is an appropriate summing up of this scene. The phrase meant 'to act the fool'. However, it could also be taken as a **metaphor** for dying in the prime of life. Some commentators feel that the Fool may be referring here to his own premature death, as he does not appear again in the play.

### Hope for the future

Despite the threat to his own life, Gloucester returns to arrange Lear's rescue, sending him to Dover where Cordelia's forces will be able to offer him 'welcome and protection' (line 91). The scene ends with Edgar's brief **soliloquy**, commenting that his own troubles seem less now that he has seen Lear's situation. Significantly, Edgar looks to the future, hopeful that one day he can emerge as himself again. For now he must 'Lurk, lurk' (line 114), keeping out of sight.

# ACT III SCENE 7

## Summary

- Cornwall sends Goneril to Albany with Gloucester's letter, containing the news of the French invasion. He expects Albany to join forces with him. Edmund accompanies Goneril as it would be inappropriate for him to be present when his father is horribly punished.

- Gloucester, who has returned to the house, is brought in and interrogated. Regan disrespectfully plucks him by the beard – a foretaste of the violence to come. Gloucester says that he sent Lear to Dover because he could not bear to see him tortured by Goneril and Regan.

- When Gloucester says he hopes to see 'The winged vengeance overtake such children' (line 64), Cornwall gouges out one of Gloucester's eyes. Regan urges her husband to pluck out his other eye.

- Appalled, one of Cornwall's own servants tries to intervene. He fatally wounds Cornwall. Regan takes a sword from another servant and runs the challenger through. In spite of his wound, Cornwall finds the strength to put out Gloucester's other eye.

- Gloucester hopes that Edmund will avenge him. Regan taunts Gloucester, informing the old man that Edmund hates him. Gloucester recognises that he has been deceived and calls on the gods to protect Edgar and forgive him for doubting his true son.

- Regan tells servants to 'thrust' Gloucester out and 'let him smell / His way to Dover' (lines 91–2). She then helps her dying husband from the stage.

- Two servants decide to help Gloucester and fetch some medicine to soothe his wounded eyes. They will take him to Poor Tom, who can act as his guide.

**A03 | KEY CONNECTION**

How the blinding of Gloucester should be staged is a matter of some controversy. Peter Brook's 1971 film sets the scene amid butchery implements and hanging joints of meat. At the moment when Cornwall leans forward to gouge out Gloucester's eye, the frame goes black, giving a strong sense that we are seeing the scene from his perspective as we hear his agonised screams.

## Analysis

### Cruelty and violence

This scene contains one of the most shocking acts of violence in any of Shakespeare's plays. There are many references to eyes and sight that increase the tension and prepare us for Gloucester's blinding, beginning with Goneril's 'Pluck out his eyes' (line 5). The verb 'pluck' has a callous, brutal quality which brings home to us the horror of the action. Even though Goneril does not take part in Gloucester's maiming, her suggestion of it implicates her in the crime. The cruelty of this scene indicates that the world has been turned upside down. One woman (a royal princess) suggests a method of torture, another relishes inflicting pain, egging her husband on to further cruelty before killing a man (the servant) herself.

As Gloucester points out, the horror is compounded by the fact that Cornwall and Regan are guests at his home. They have little respect for the rules of civilised behaviour. It is true that Cornwall decides not to kill Gloucester in the absence of a trial (needing 'the form of justice', line 25), as this might rouse opinion against him, but he seems to believe that he is powerful enough to be able to torture and mutilate Gloucester with impunity.

**A03 | KEY CONNECTION**

Cornwall's sickening line, 'Upon these eyes of thine I'll set my foot' (line 66) suggests he may gouge out Gloucester's eyes and squash them with his boot. Traditionally, Gloucester's chair has been faced away from the audience to hide exactly what happens, but since Peter Brook's stage production of 1962, some directors have allowed the action to be seen, often adopting Brook's method of having Cornwall use a spur on his boot to grind out Gloucester's eyes.

**KEY CONTEXT**

Gloucester's rebuke to Regan, 'Naughty lady' (line 37), may sound like an extraordinary understatement to today's audiences, who are likely to associate the word 'naughty' with small children. In the seventeenth century, however, 'naughty' had a stronger sense. 'Naught' meant 'nothing' and by extension 'morally worthless', so Gloucester is actually accusing her of behaving in an evil way.

**KEY INTERPRETATION**

Critic David Scott Kastan argues that Shakespeare's tragedies offer us 'emotional truth', not answers to philosophical questions about the origins and meaning of suffering. Although the characters try to explain their plight, the story always goes on to undercut these explanations. 'Tragedy, for Shakespeare, is the genre of uncompensated suffering.'

## Gloucester's suffering and heroism

Like Lear, Gloucester achieves heroism through suffering. Like Kent, he suffers because he has tried to help Lear. In this scene, which contains some of his most powerful speeches in the play, Gloucester is eloquent, brave and determined as he defends himself and castigates Cornwall and Regan for their cruelty to the king. The Earl becomes the voice of the audience, describing their outrage. Like Lear, Gloucester learns the truth about his children in a particularly brutal way. He also shares Lear's agony when he discovers that he has been taken in by outward appearances. The barbarism of the whole scene is summed up by Regan's final callous order to the servants.

# Study focus: The decency of the servants

It is noticeable that the servants do not share their master's brutally careless attitude towards right and wrong. Cornwall has to tell them twice to tie Gloucester to the chair, indicating that they are reluctant to behave brutally towards him. The anonymous servant who stands up to Cornwall, telling him 'better service have I never done you / Than now to bid you hold' (lines 72–3) is a servant in the spirit of Kent, ready to give his honest opinion when he sees his master do ill, rather than being a mere yes-man like Oswald. At the end of the scene, in a section omitted from the Folio text, it is the servants who take advantage of Cornwall and Regan's absence to treat Gloucester's eyes and find him a guide.

Although the play has reached its lowest point before the tragic final scene, the generous actions of the servants indicate that there is still some kind of justice at work. In modern productions of the play, the interval usually occurs at the end of the scene, giving the audience time to reflect on what has gone before, and also allowing the squeamish to slip out early.

# Key quotation: A fitting punishment for Gloucester?

It is Goneril's suggestion that, as Cornwall now has Gloucester in his power, he should 'Pluck out his eyes' (line 5). Blinding had been a medieval punishment for rape, perhaps because sight was held to be a key sense in provoking men to lust. While Goneril probably has no deeper intention than devising a random act of violence, Edgar later comes to think his father deserved such a punishment for committing adultery (V.3.172–3).

It can also be argued that it is a fitting punishment for Gloucester because he failed to see the truth about his sons, mistaking appearance for reality and as a result threatening the harmless Edgar with death (a threat Edgar has clearly not forgotten). Gloucester's tragedy, like Lear's, is not that he is an innocent victim but that his punishment is so extreme and merciless.

# ACT IV SCENE 1

## Summary

- Edgar reflects on being a poor, despised outcast. Although he comforts himself that he cannot sink any lower, his fragile optimism is shattered when his father is led on, blinded and in despair.

- Gloucester wishes to find Edgar, so that he can ask for his forgiveness. He offers a dark view of life: 'As flies to wanton boys are we to th'Gods; / They kill us for their sport' (lines 36–7).

- Edgar, as Poor Tom, agrees to lead Gloucester to Dover. Edgar is still distressed and has difficulty in maintaining his disguise.

- Like Lear, Gloucester is now preoccupied by thoughts of justice. His final speech conveys his desire to die. He promises Edgar further payment if he leads him 'to the very brim' (line 75) of a cliff at Dover. We understand that he intends to jump from the cliff and kill himself.

## Analysis

### Endurance and despair

At the start of the scene, Edgar seems to feel positive, his experiences have taught him to withstand the 'blasts' (line 9) of Fortune. He is learning to endure whatever he encounters, though the sight of his mutilated father is a severe challenge. Gloucester's own resilience is severely tested in Act IV Scene 1. Are we to accept his view of the sadistic gods as an accurate description of the world of *King Lear*? Or is his pessimism just a reflection of his current state of mind?

## Study focus: Gloucester's progress

Even at his most desolate, Gloucester acts generously towards others, speaking graciously to the old man who leads him on and to Poor Tom. He seems more concerned with their fortunes than with his own. If the gods are cruel, this scene proves that man can be kind. Gloucester's interest in social justice reflects Lear's, and proves that the patriarchs have learned to see the world more clearly. As Gloucester says so aptly, he 'stumbled' (line 19) when he saw.

For Gloucester, clarity of vision also brings despair. He wishes to reach Dover, not to rendezvous with Cordelia and her forces, but to end his life. Edgar's role in this scene is to guide our responses to his father's misery. His final statement, 'Poor Tom shall lead thee' (line 79), has a double meaning. He will lead his father to Dover but he will also try to lead him out of despair.

**A01** **PROGRESS BOOSTER**

Remember that *King Lear* is a play, not a novel. When discussing the significance of a quotation, try to consider how the actor might have spoken their lines and their behaviour as they did so. In this scene, for example, does Gloucester stand resignedly and mutter his lines as though stunned, or is he agitated, snapping out the words in a tone of bitterness?

**A04** **KEY CONNECTION**

In Akira Kurosawa's Japanese film *Ran* (1985), which is partly based on *King Lear*, Gloucester's despairing view of the gods is expressed by a character called Kyoami, but immediately corrected for the audience by another called Tango, who brands it an evasion of human responsibility. He says, 'Do not blaspheme! It is the gods who weep ... They can't save us from ourselves.'

**KEY CONTEXT**

When Albany condemns Goneril's treatment of her father, she replies, 'the text is foolish' (line 37). Even though the play is set in pagan times, the original audience would surely identify Albany's criticism of Goneril for condemning her own 'origin' as a reference to the first of the Ten Commandments, something which no Christian would consider foolish: 'Honour thy father and thy mother: that thy days may be long in the land which the Lord thy God giveth thee' (Exodus 20:12).

## ACT IV SCENE 2

### Summary

- When Goneril and Edmund return to Albany's castle, Oswald tells her that Albany has undergone a change of heart. Goneril says her husband is a coward and that she must now take command. She tells Edmund to return to Cornwall to help prepare for battle. Goneril says that she will shortly become Edmund's lover.

- Albany appears and Goneril greets him sarcastically. In return, Albany says she is a devil and that the sisters have behaved like 'Tigers, not daughters' (line 40). His language becomes increasingly violent as he describes how he would like to tear Goneril limb from limb.

- A messenger arrives with the news that Cornwall is dead. Albany greets this as an act of justice. The messenger also has a letter from Regan for Goneril. Goneril is suspicious of her sister. She is concerned that the widowed Regan will seek to marry Edmund.

- On learning that Edmund collaborated in his father's torment, Albany resolves to revenge Gloucester and support Lear's cause.

### Analysis

### Study focus: Albany becomes a figure of justice

Look closely at Albany's role in this scene. The change in Albany suggests that the power of the evil characters will no longer go unchecked. He becomes a figure of justice and morality, voicing the audience's disgust. He tells Goneril bluntly that she is worthless: 'You are not worth the dust which the rude wind / Blows in your face' (lines 30–1). He says that her actions will inevitably lead to her own destruction. When he hears at the end of the scene of Gloucester's blinding, he promises to take 'revenge' (line 96).

**PROGRESS BOOSTER**

While some characters like Oswald are static, others develop considerably through the play. When writing about Albany, for example, avoid simplistic statements about his behaviour and trace instead how, as he throws off his wife's influence, he moves from the ineffectual figure of Act I Scene 4 through the angry moralist of the present scene to the decisive commander of Act V Scene 3.

### Goneril schemes to take charge

Goneril dismisses Albany as a coward and a weakling. She continues to assume authority, urging her husband to repel the French invasion while secretly wooing Edmund, whom she desires to be her sexual and political partner. Since this would not be possible if she was still married to Albany, there is an implication – which becomes clearer later in the play – that the pair will murder Albany.

### Key quotation: Evil is self-destructive

Albany tells Goneril: 'She that herself will sliver and disbranch / From her material sap, perforce must wither / And come to deadly use' (lines 34–6). He is telling her that if she behaves unnaturally she will unleash forces that will destroy her. In overthrowing her father, he argues, she is like a branch that rips itself away from a tree only to become dead wood, fit merely for the fire.

# ACT IV SCENE 3

## Summary

- Kent asks a Gentleman why the King of France has returned home. We learn that he had urgent state business to attend to.
- Kent asks the Gentleman how Cordelia reacted when she read his letters describing Lear's treatment at the hands of Goneril and Regan. We are told that 'holy water' fell from her 'heavenly eyes' (line 30) as she cried for Lear's plight.
- Kent reports Lear's arrival in Dover. The king is sometimes in a better frame of mind, but even when in this state he is so ashamed of his 'unkindness' (line 42) to Cordelia that he does not wish to see her.
- The Gentleman says that Albany and Cornwall's forces are on the move. Kent takes him to attend on Lear.

## Analysis

### Cordelia's return

This scene was not included in the Folio version of the play (see ***King Lear*: A Snapshot, Textual problems**) so is not in all editions. The scene prepares us for Cordelia's return. Just as the Gentleman's description of Lear in the storm in Act III Scene 1 prepares us to picture a raging tempest in the next scene, so this Gentleman's description of Cordelia prepares us to look upon the actor in the next scene (a boy would have played the part in Shakespeare's theatre) as the epitome of graceful, Christian femininity, compassionate and loving.

## Study focus: Lear's shame **A02**

We know that the reconciliation between Lear and Cordelia will be a painful and poignant one. Lear has started to regain his wits, but clarity of vision brings with it distress. He feels 'burning shame' (line 47) for the way he has treated Cordelia. Kent quickly recaps these misdeeds for the audience: Lear has withdrawn his love from Cordelia, dismissed her to an uncertain life abroad and given what should rightly have been hers to her ruthless sisters. Father and daughter now share the same emotion: sorrow. The reference to the armies of Albany and Cornwall, moving south to confront Cordelia's French forces, ensures that we do not lose sight of the bigger story.

## Key quotation: Animal imagery **A02**

Kent describes Regan and Goneril as Lear's 'dog-hearted daughters' (line 45).

Throughout the play animal **imagery** is used, not only to characterise the evil sisters, but to draw attention to any behaviour that is driven by the self-centred physical appetites which human beings share with animals. In Act I Scene 4, Lear compares Goneril to a sea monster (line 260), a bird of prey (261), a snake (287) and a wolf (307). In this scene, in contrast, Cordelia is praised for her self-control (lines 13–4) and her tears are called 'holy water' (line 30), suggesting that she rises above mere animal desires and sees life from a more developed moral perspective.

**A03** **KEY CONTEXT**

Why was this scene cut from the later, Folio version of the play? An English audience might well be uncomfortable at seeing a French army invade their country, even in support of Cordelia. Some people think that for this reason the Folio version downplays the French presence. With references to the French king and 'Monsieur La Far' removed, the invaders become a military force led by Cordelia, even if the French king may have supplied her with troops, and not the regular French army launching an attack on England.

# ACT IV SCENES 4–5

## Summary

- Cordelia describes how Lear has been seen, out of control, wearing a crown of flowers and weeds. A doctor tells her that Lear might be cured by sleep, which can be induced by sedatives. She sends soldiers out to find Lear.
- A messenger informs her that the British army is drawing closer. To allay any fears the audience might have of a foreign invasion, Cordelia insists that she has come to defend Lear's rights; she is motivated by love, not by political ambition.
- Regan asks Oswald why Goneril has written to Edmund. She tries to persuade him to show her the letter he is carrying. She remarks that it was a mistake to let Gloucester live: his cruel treatment has turned people against them.
- When Oswald insists that he must leave, Regan adopts a more aggressive tone. She and Edmund have talked, and agreed on marriage. Goneril must be warned off.
- Regan gives Oswald a letter or gift for Edmund and asks him to deliver it. She casually mentions the fact that there is a reward for anyone who kills Gloucester.

## Analysis

### Cordelia's compassion for Lear

Lear's crown, made of weeds and flowers which flourish in the English summer, has symbolic significance in Scene 4. The king is now associated with enduring nature rather than the artificial, inward-looking world of the court, fittingly given his interest in justice and the human condition. Cordelia shows great compassion. Like Edgar, she actively assists the parent who cruelly rejected her, sending a hundred soldiers to find him (a 'century', line 6). If they gather together to escort him to her, he will in effect have regained the hundred knights of which he was deprived by her sisters.

### Progress booster: Contrasting groups of characters

Make sure you can comment on how Shakespeare contrasts groups of characters in the play. Regan's preoccupation with her own selfish lust in Scene 5 contrasts sharply with Cordelia's generosity in the previous scene. Throughout Act IV, Lear's daughters are juxtaposed. We watch the progress of both good and evil. The language Regan uses to describe her liaison with Edmund is entirely in keeping with the materialistic desires of the evil characters; Edmund is 'more convenient' (line 31) for her than for Goneril. It seems that Goneril and Regan are now divided by their rivalry for Edmund's love. In some modern productions Regan even strokes or kisses Oswald at the words 'I'll love thee much' (line 21), though as a princess speaking to a servant she is more likely to be offering him a financial reward. Albany's reluctance to assist the conniving sisters may be hinted at in the comment that he has only brought his army to fight the French 'with much ado' (line 2). Meanwhile, the good characters share common aims and appear to be gathering strength. The fact that people are appalled by Gloucester's blinding also suggests that we might be justified in hoping that evil will be vanquished.

---

**KEY CONNECTION**    A04

Readings of Cordelia's character which suggest that she is a Christ-like figure rest on her words, 'O dear father! / It is thy business that I go about' (lines 23–4 of Scene 4), which echo Christ's in Luke 2: 49, 'I must go about my father's business'.

# ACT IV SCENE 6

## Summary

- Edgar leads Gloucester to Dover. He pretends they are going up a steep hill to a cliff edge. Gloucester throws himself off the imaginary cliff. Pretending now to be a passerby on the beach, Edgar tells him his companion was a devil and he must have been preserved by a miracle. Gloucester accepts that he should no longer seek to die before his time.
- Lear enters, wearing his crown of weeds. He mistakes Gloucester for Goneril 'with a white beard' (line 96) and launches into a tirade against female sexuality. Lear's fear of monstrous femininity also leads him to introduce the topic of Gloucester's adultery. There is a cruel **irony** in Lear's lines about Gloucester's 'kind' bastard son.
- Lear has become obsessed with social and moral justice. Authority is a sham, he concludes: even a dog would be obeyed if it held the right social position. He disparages rich sinners who are able to defy justice, while beggars cannot escape punishment for their crimes because they have no money for bribes.
- Lear advises Gloucester to get glasses so that he can act like a cunning politician, pretending to see things which will justify his actions. He finally recognises his friend, telling him to be patient and advising him that it is man's lot to suffer and endure.
- When Cordelia's attendants arrive, Lear runs off. Edgar asks for news of the battle expected between the French and British forces. He begins to lead Gloucester to a safe place.
- Oswald comes upon them, delighted that he will be able to kill Gloucester and claim Regan's reward. Gloucester welcomes the prospect of death. Assuming the accent of a country bumpkin, Edgar challenges Oswald, whom he fatally wounds in the fight.
- In his dying speech Oswald asks Edgar to take the letters he is carrying to Edmund. Edgar instead reads the letters and discovers Goneril's plot against Albany's life. Shocked, he decides to inform Albany of the contents of the letter when the time is right. He drags Oswald's body offstage for burial, then returns to escort his father to safety. A drum roll suggests battle is imminent.

## Analysis

### Study focus: Edgar's feelings

 **A02**

Some people have felt uneasy at the way Edgar conceals his identity from Gloucester and tricks him at Dover. Is his attempt to look after his injured father contaminated by any contrary feelings? It has been suggested that Edgar simply doesn't know how to speak to his father after what has happened to them both. It could also be that part of him remains angry about how his father believed Edmund and tried to have him hunted down. How do you interpret Edgar's feelings?

**A05** KEY INTERPRETATION

Gloucester's attempt to jump off a non-existent cliff runs the risk of provoking confusion or laughter in the audience. In different productions the actors playing Gloucester have variously fallen forwards, jumped into the air or even been caught, then lowered to the ground, by Edgar. How would you stage this action to best show Gloucester's despair and Edgar's anxiety for him?

**A05** KEY INTERPRETATION

'They fight, and Edgar knocks him down' – this stage direction takes only a moment to read, but we should not be misled into thinking that the script requires only a brief scuffle between Edgar and Oswald. This is a key moment in the story, when Edgar at last fights back against the forces of evil and demonstrates his love for his father, and he does so armed with only a stick against an opponent with a sword. We should probably expect a prolonged battle in which Edgar shows his mettle but comes alarmingly close to being killed until, in a sudden twist, he grabs a dagger or even the sword itself from Oswald and drives it into him.

**KEY CONTEXT**

Throughout Lear's mental disturbance, the virtuous characters continue to address him respectfully as their sovereign. Critics have suggested that this deference is proof that Shakespeare does not seek to undermine conventional ideas about kingship in this play.

**KEY CONTEXT** A03

There are various theories about why Shakespeare included the Gloucester **subplot**. Two practical reasons have been put forward. Firstly, the Lear plot did not have sufficient roles for the actors in Shakespeare's company, the King's Men, and secondly, audiences were accustomed to double plots which made the action of the play more varied and lively.

### Edgar guides our responses

Edgar's description of the view from the cliff top serves two purposes: to convince his father that he stands on the edge of the cliff and to show us Gloucester's desperation. His **aside** at lines 33–4 hints at the terror created by Gloucester's attempted suicide, which can seem both tragic and absurd in performance. Once Lear is on stage, Edgar says very little, offering brief asides. His words (lines 85 and 140) emphasise the **pathos** of the exchange between Lear and Gloucester.

### Lear's obsession with justice

Both patriarchs seem worn out, but they 'see how this world goes' (lines 148–9). They have achieved understanding and wisdom through suffering. Lear now seems to be playing the same role for Gloucester that the Fool played for him. He is a cruel commentator in this scene. His obsession with justice fits in with his earlier concern for 'unaccommodated man' (III.4.109). His crown of weeds and flowers reminds us of his kingly appearance in Act I Scene 1, but his experiences since then have shown him that authority is easy to abuse, especially when a powerful person is surrounded by flatterers as he once was.

### Edgar the revenger

At the end of the scene, Edgar takes on a more active role when he defends his father and kills Oswald. His adoption of a country accent here lulls Oswald into a false sense of security. We saw in Act II Scene 2 that Oswald was scared to fight Kent, but now he is motivated by reward money and believes his opponents to be simply an old blind man and an ignorant yokel. As an aristocrat, Edgar is actually an experienced swordsman. In many productions Edgar snatches a dagger from Oswald. Edgar's expertise in fighting prepares us for his role of revenger in Act V Scene 3.

## Progress booster: Master of suspense

While it is helpful to focus on themes and characterisation, never forget that Shakespeare is a dramatist; try to comment on his use of suspense to engage us with the events of the play.

One of the chief tasks of a storyteller is to keep the audience or reader wondering what will happen next. Shakespeare is a master of suspenseful storytelling and often keeps his audience on the edge of their seats with multiple storylines. In this scene we wonder at various times whether Edgar can preserve Gloucester from suicide, whether Cordelia will be reunited with Lear, what will happen when the British and French forces meet and whether Edgar will be able to take revenge on Edmund. Amidst these ongoing questions comes the sudden shock of the fight with Oswald.

## Revision task 4: Does Lear remain at the play's centre?

'By the end of Act IV, the focus of the drama has switched from Lear to Edgar.'

How far do you agree with this statement? List as many reasons for and against it as you can.

# ACT IV SCENE 7

## Summary

- Lear has been brought to the French camp near Dover. The old king is carried on in a chair and the Doctor calls for music to awaken him.
- When Lear wakes, he is bewildered and thinks he is in hell, 'bound / Upon a wheel of fire' (line 47). At first he does not seem to recognise Cordelia, who asks for his blessing. Lear then falls on his knees before Cordelia, showing that he regrets wronging her. He sees himself clearly as 'a very foolish fond old man' (line 60).
- Cordelia denies that she has any reason to feel bitter towards her father. Father and daughter leave the stage together.
- Kent and the Gentleman remain behind to discuss the battle. Edmund has been put in charge of Cornwall's men. A bloody confrontation is expected.

## Analysis

### Study focus: Pathos and renewal  **A02**

This is a scene of pathos and renewal. Kent says that he will not put off his disguise yet because it would spoil his plans, but a likelier reason, suggested by the director Harley Granville Barker, is that Shakespeare wants to focus all our attention on the moving reunion of Cordelia and Lear. Sleep and music were understood to have powerful healing properties. Our sense of restoration is heightened when the characters kneel before Lear, who is once again treated as a powerful monarch. All the words addressed to him are respectful and he sits 'above' his subjects once more, as he did in Act I Scene 1.

### Lear humbles himself

We soon realise that Lear is not the towering figure he once was. His speeches are hesitant and confused. At first he does not recognise Cordelia and thinks that he may have arrived in the afterlife. His misconception that he is in France may be due to the sight of French flags and costumes, or simply a recollection that Cordelia married the French king. Once he recognises her, Lear humbles himself before Cordelia. He no longer speaks of himself as the royal 'we'. Lear understands that he sinned against his youngest daughter and wishes to honour her.

### Lear a victim

Lear does not accept any responsibility for Goneril and Regan. They are identified (in Cordelia's lines before Lear awakes) as the sole cause of the king's suffering. We are expected to view Lear now as a victim. Certainly, this is the view Lear himself holds. His lines are full of self-pity. This scene (which is heavily cut in the Folio version of the play) comes as an immense relief after the chaos and darkness of Acts III and IV, although news of the battle suggests the harmony that is achieved here is already under threat.

**A03** **KEY CONTEXT**

For centuries it was believed that music was based on the divine harmony which shaped the universe, causing it to have healing properties for the mind and spirit. Psychologists today still make use of music therapy, though without cosmological beliefs. The powerful healing properties of music are shown in a number of Shakespeare's plays, including the late romance, *The Winter's Tale*.

**A04** **KEY CONNECTION**

In the 1980 TV film, the reunion of Cordelia and Lear is uplit from the snowy-white sheets under which Lear lies sleeping. His vulnerability is symbolised by the fact that his beard has been shaved off – perhaps allying him with the beard-plucked Gloucester in the blinding scene.

# EXTRACT ANALYSIS: IV.7.30–84

This quiet and moving scene comes as a relief after the violent struggles of Act III, and the harsh comedy of Gloucester and Lear's final meeting in Act IV Scene 6. We are prepared for the scene of reconciliation by Kent's conversation with the Gentleman in Act IV Scene 3, where we learned that Lear was so ashamed of 'his own unkindness' that he would not see Cordelia (IV.3.42). Other dramatic devices also point towards restoration. Music is being played, and as Lear is carried in wearing fresh garments, all the characters on stage fall to their knees, reaffirming Lear's status as king. Cordelia kneels at her father's side and kisses his hand. This gesture of love and pity sets the tone for the scene to come.

Cordelia's speech at line 30 is her last long speech in the play. Her sole concern is Lear. As she describes Lear's sufferings in the storm we are reminded of Goneril and Regan's cruelty. We are further reminded how far the '*poor perdu*' (line 34) has fallen when Cordelia laments the way her father was forced to find a hovel full of 'short and musty straw' (line 40). These sorrowful descriptions highlight Lear's vulnerability and reaffirm Cordelia's virtuous nature. Her warmth and compassion contrast sharply with her sisters' cold vindictiveness. Cordelia's modesty is shown when she asks the Doctor to speak to Lear first. She seems as reluctant to speak now as she was in Act I Scene 1. Are we to assume that Cordelia still finds it hard to express her love? Perhaps she shrinks from speaking because she is nervous about how her 'child-changed' (line 17) father will react when he sees her.

When Lear wakes up, Cordelia's anxious questions, 'How does my royal Lord? How fares your Majesty?' (line 44) indicate that she now submits to her father's authority. The formal distance of these words is softened by the possessive 'my', which suggests Cordelia's desire to re-establish a close relationship with Lear. She urgently wants to be recognised and is upset when she realises her father is 'Still, still, far wide' (line 50). She continues to seem choked for the rest of the scene, falling to her knees and begging for Lear's blessing, and then weeping during Lear's hesitant self-appraisal at line 60. After this she is so overwrought that she can only offer a brief 'No cause, no cause' (line 75) and ask gently if her father will take a walk with her (but only if it pleases him).

In Act IV Scene 7 Cordelia seems to be the perfect, doting daughter. Her submissiveness suggests to some modern critics that Shakespeare has started to rehabilitate and reaffirm patriarchal hierarchy in the final scenes of the play. Cordelia's insistence that she has no reason to hate Lear confirms, perhaps, that the authority he exercised over her in Act I Scene 1 has now been accepted as just. Alternatively, we might see her gentle pity as redemptive, and her 'No cause, no cause' as the natural response of a caring daughter.

**KEY INTERPRETATION** **A05**

Many would argue that *King Lear* is an unusual kind of **tragedy** because, instead of seeing a good but flawed man fall (as in *Othello*), we watch as a tyrant moves towards a conciliatory ending, where he is reunited with the person he loves most.

**KEY CONTEXT** **A03**

From 1788 to 1820 *King Lear* was banned from the British stage, because the king at that time, George III, was suffering from mental problems and audiences might find the depiction of Lear to be either amusing or in bad taste. This reminds us that, to audiences of past centuries, a distressed king would have seemed a far more alarming and important topic than it does today, in an era of constitutional monarchs and republics.

Lear's lines indicate that the king is now a figure of **pathos**. His first speech shows his relentless suffering:

You do me wrong to take me out o' th'grave;
Thou art a soul in bliss; but I am bound
Upon a wheel of fire, that mine own tears
Do scald like molten lead. (lines 45–8)

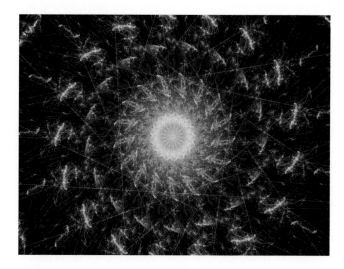

He is weeping and is utterly bewildered by what he sees. He cannot piece together the events of the previous twenty-four hours and murmurs helplessly, 'I know not what to say'. Perhaps Lear has learned the lesson that Cordelia was trying to teach him in Act I Scene 1, that language cannot be expected to express emotions truly. He has certainly been humbled by his experiences.

Although Lear continues to speak about himself in a self-pitying tone, he looks outwards too. He says that he would hate 'To see another thus' (line 54) and expresses doubts about his senses. He sums himself up with devastating simplicity; he is 'a very foolish fond old man … not in my perfect mind'. Most significantly, he attempts to kneel before Cordelia and recognises that she has 'some cause' for hating him. It might also be argued that Lear's use of first person pronouns, 'methinks' and 'I', suggests greater humility. Gone is the earlier use of the omnipotent third person, the royal 'we'. Lear seems to have accepted his diminished status. He shuns anything that suggests regality, denying that he has any authority. He is more concerned now with 'my child Cordelia' (line 70). Here we are being prepared for Act V Scene 3, when Lear acts out the role of protective father. When he offers to drink poison even the most hard-hearted spectator will be moved. Lear's self-pity seems acceptable because he has suffered so deeply.

We are pulled in two ways in this scene. Cordelia and Lear express the same emotions: pain, humility, concern. Cordelia constantly tries to reassure her father, as at line 75. When they leave the stage together it seems that the reconciliation is complete. Lear has finally achieved his heart's desire; he can now rely on Cordelia's 'kind nursery' (I.1.123). This outcome provides us with a sense of relief. But we also doubt that Lear will survive long. He no longer speaks or acts like a mighty king. Every line he delivers confirms his weakness. Fresh garments cannot restore Lear to his former glory. His own view of himself is altogether more realistic than the version of Lear to which Cordelia responds. Cordelia's reverence is ultimately rather hopeless.

This scene is significant because we see a fragile family harmony restored. Lear no longer holds false values. He recognises love and goodness accurately. We welcome his increased wisdom and humility. Act IV Scene 7 also provides an outlet for the pity we have felt for the old king since the end of Act II. Finally, this scene points towards the restoration of the hierarchy that occurs at the end of *King Lear*. As the play moves into Act V, we wait anxiously to see whether Cordelia's virtues or Goneril and Regan's vices will triumph.

**A03** **KEY CONTEXT**

In previous versions of the story – including the earlier play *The True Chronicle History of King Lear and his Daughters* – Lear and Cordelia are reunited and the king restored to the throne. (Events take a turn for the worse after Lear's death in many versions, but the *Chronicle* play does not take the story that far.) It seems that Shakespeare is drawing deliberately on his audience's optimistic expectations in order to dash their hopes in the bleak conclusion.

## ACT V SCENES 1–2

### Summary

- Preparations for the battle are underway. Regan fears that Edmund may love Goneril. When Albany and Goneril arrive with their forces, Goneril tells us she would rather lose the battle than lose Edmund.
- Albany sympathises with Cordelia's cause, but agrees to fight the invaders. As he is about to follow the others off, Edgar appears (still disguised). He gives Albany the letter he found on Oswald and tells him to open it before going into battle. He asks Albany to have a trumpet sounded if the British win the battle – this will summon a noble warrior who will confront Edmund and Goneril over their treachery.
- Edmund knows the sisters are such rivals for his love that one will have to die in order for him to 'enjoy' the other. He decides to wait and see what happens in the battle. Although Albany intends to show mercy to Lear and Cordelia if the British win, Edmund plans to kill them.
- Edgar takes Gloucester to a safe place while the battle rages. He returns with the news that the French have lost. Lear and Cordelia have been captured.
- Overcome by negative thoughts, Gloucester refuses to move further. Edgar chides him, saying that, although he should prepare himself for death, it is not for him to choose the moment. Gloucester allows himself to be led away.

### Analysis

**KEY INTERPRETATION**

Edmund has been described as the 'wittiest and most attractive of villains' and 'a cheery swashbuckler who could engage the audience's complicit laughter'. Do you agree with these assessments? Do you find your view of him changes as the play progresses?

### Study focus: Edmund and his allies

**A02**

Note the uneasiness and urgency displayed in Act V Scene 1. Goneril and Regan's feud over Edmund continues, Goneril and Albany are at odds, and Albany and Edmund clearly share different intentions about the battle and its outcome. Edmund's brief responses to Regan suggest his impatience with talk of love. In his first **soliloquy** he reveals his approach to marriage, which matches the ruthlessness he has shown in all his dealings with others. His only loyalty is to himself. His last three lines suggest that Edmund revels in his newly exalted position. We fear the outcome of the battle and wonder how the rivalry between Goneril and Regan will be resolved.

### A time of death and danger

The battle in Scene 2 occurs off stage. Shakespeare is most interested in its consequences. We get an indication of what is to occur in the final scene when Edgar says, 'Men must endure / Their going hence, even as their coming hither: / Ripeness is all' (lines 9–11). Gloucester wishes to die, and we know that Lear is in great danger. Both men have endured more than enough. The **tragic** stoicism of these lines prepares us for the outcome of Act V Scene 3.

### Revision task 5: Conflict among the usurpers

Goneril, Regan and Edmund, along with their reluctant ally Albany, are challenged by people loyal to Lear and by their own internal divisions. Make notes on what each of them wants and how this turns them against one another.

# ACT V SCENE 3

## Summary

- Lear comforts Cordelia. Edmund sends them to prison with a secret death warrant. He resists Albany's demands to hand the prisoners over.

- Regan announces her intention of marrying Edmund, but Albany arrests Edmund for treason, then has the trumpet sounded to summon Edmund's accuser. Meanwhile, we learn that Goneril has poisoned Regan. Edgar appears, disguised and armed. Edmund agrees to fight him and is fatally wounded.

- Albany confronts Goneril with her letter to Edmund. After a last desperate attempt to assert her power, she runs off. Edmund confesses his crimes. He says he will forgive his adversary if he is a nobleman. Edgar at last puts aside his disguise.

- Edgar describes how Gloucester was overcome and died when he finally revealed his true identity to him. We learn that Goneril has killed herself and Regan has died from the poison. Kent arrives to see Lear. Albany urgently asks Edmund where he sent Lear and Cordelia. They try to establish how to cancel the death warrant.

- Edmund is carried off to die. Lear comes in carrying Cordelia, hoping desperately that his daughter still breathes. We learn that Lear killed Cordelia's hangman.

- As Lear's senses fail, a messenger brings news that Edmund has died. Kent tells Edgar to leave Lear be. He will welcome death after the sufferings of his life. He adds that he too expects to die soon. Lear dies, perhaps believing that Cordelia still lives.

- Edgar becomes the new ruler. He says the survivors 'Shall never see so much nor live so long' (line 326), suggesting that the lives of those who remain have been shattered.

## Analysis

### The evil are punished

Events occur swiftly, dominated by violent deaths and sorrow. There is a brief moment of hope when Lear imagines his life with Cordelia in prison, reinstating his goal from Act I Scene 1 to unburden himself of his cares and spend his time with his favourite daughter. Almost immediately, however, we learn of Edmund's plan to have the pair killed. Arguably, Edmund is responsible for the deaths of the whole royal family, as well as his father's fate. His own death is, as Edgar suggests, richly deserved. In fact Edmund is doomed as soon as Albany has sent away his troops, leaving him isolated (lines 103–5). The audience may be pleased that Edmund is killed by Edgar rather than Albany, since Edgar has so much reason to take revenge, yet the spectacle of one brother killing another is still a deeply shocking one.

The deaths of Goneril and Regan are similarly well deserved but repulsive. In a world where the king has lost control of his court, fathers of their children and individuals of their desires, indiscriminate destruction has been let loose which now at last overwhelms those who caused it, bringing the tragic process to its terrible conclusion.

**A03** **KEY CONTEXT**

Some critics feel that the final scene ends on a faintly optimistic note. Edgar was the name of a king who united England and Scotland, so if Gloucester's son is now in charge, perhaps reunification of Lear's battered kingdom is possible. Edgar's experience of staying silent, trusting no one and striking only when the time is right will have equipped him with self-control, wariness and patience, qualities which Lear certainly did not possess.

**A03** **KEY CONTEXT**

The last lines of the play are attributed differently in the Quarto and Folio versions of the text. In the Quarto (the earlier version of the play), Albany speaks the final lines. In the Folio, the same lines are given to Edgar. Usually, in Shakespeare's plays, the highest ranking surviving figure speaks the closing lines. So, if Edgar speaks the lines, there is a definite sense that there has been a shift in power.

### An ending without hope?

The audience may be pleased that Edmund, Regan, Goneril and Oswald have all paid for their misdeeds with their lives, but the destruction does not end there. Although the good characters draw together and assert themselves, they are unable to save Lear, Cordelia or Gloucester. Lear and Gloucester certainly bear some responsibility for unleashing the forces of evil, and even Cordelia can be criticised for defying her father so bluntly and publicly, but the punishment visited on all three seems horribly out of proportion to their misdeeds.

It is difficult to find any sense of hope in the final doleful lines of the play. Edgar does not look forward to the new reign, but having reluctantly taken on the role of king, focuses his thoughts on 'this sad time' (line 323). We are left exhausted and numb, like the characters.

**KEY CONTEXT** **A03**

We are bound to respond to Cordelia's death in terms of the play's tragic themes, but if Cordelia had lived to become queen it might have raised quite different issues for Shakespeare's original audience. Many people had reservations about female rule, and few would be happy with the accession of a queen who was married to the King of France, threatening possible French control of Britain. In contrast, Edgar has the qualities needed to be a strong, resilient ruler and his acceptance of the crown at the play's conclusion leaves Britain in a safe pair of hands.

# Study focus: Lear as tragic hero

Kent has no desire to live after his master has lost the battle, and when Lear appears with Cordelia in his arms we know that optimism of any kind is out of place. However often we have seen the play, the death of Cordelia and the final passing of Lear create a sense of bitter disappointment and shocking injustice. Yet even at this stage of the play Lear achieves a heroic status by killing Cordelia's assassin and struggling to preserve her life as his own life slips away. We must agree with Kent's assessment that Lear will find a welcome release in death. Like Gloucester, he dies feeling both joy and pain.

Although the forces of good triumph through Edgar and Albany, the drama focuses on Lear. Albany tries to assume control and put events into a positive perspective, but is forced to break off ('O! see, see!', line 304) at the sight of Lear lamenting over Cordelia's body. Lear has been through extremes of human experience and suffered unreasonably, yet emerges as a larger-than-life figure, still struggling to understand his plight. It is this emphasis on a fallible human being grappling with overwhelming challenges which gives the play its **tragic** power.

## Key quotation: Divine justice?  **A02**

When he overcomes Edmund, Edgar proclaims, 'The Gods are just' (line 170). He gives as an example of their justice his father's blinding, claiming that this was a fit punishment for committing adultery. Modern audiences are unlikely to take Edgar's harsh words at face value. Nonetheless, we may have some sympathy for his resentment of his father, endorse his sense of triumph at defeating Edmund and suspect that his belief in the gods will help make him a strong, confident king.

Some critics have argued that the play actually depicts a godless world, others that a sense of divine justice is present and helps shape the conclusion. What is your view?

# PROGRESS CHECK

## Section One: Check your understanding

These tasks will help you to evaluate your knowledge and skills level in this particular area.

1. How far in your view is Lear responsible for his own downfall? Make a list of key points for and against his responsibility.

2. Cordelia's refusal to speak lovingly to her father in Act I Scene 1 and her later invasion of Britain could be seen as key factors creating **tragedy**. Make notes on how Shakespeare's presentation of these events seeks to place Cordelia in a good light.

3. What precisely are Goneril and Regan's complaints about their father? Make notes on how far you sympathise with them.

4. How does the Duke of Kent contribute to the development of the story? List how he affects the other characters and how he aids our understanding.

5. Break down the stages of Lear's 'madness'. Begin by considering whether he shows any signs of senility in the opening scene of the play.

6. Make notes on how Edmund convinces Gloucester that Edgar is plotting against him.

7. Some critics consider Goneril and Regan virtually interchangeable. Make notes on any differences between them which you can find.

8. What is the Fool trying to make Lear realise? Take three examples of what he says and explain their significance.

9. The actor Brian Cox was struck by how many questions he had to ask when playing Lear. List five questions that Lear asks during the play and comment on what they reveal about him.

10. Why is the storm scene (Act III Scene 1) important? Note three key aspects.

11. Shakespeare includes soliloquies of some length at I.2.1–22, I.2.121–41, II.2.156–69, II.3.1–21, III.6.101–14 and V.1.55–69. Choose three of these and make notes on what the audience learns from them.

12. Sum up the differences between Lear's and Edmund's views of nature.

13. The play is set in pre-Christian times. Find three references to the pagan gods and comment on how an audience might respond to each of them.

14. What is the symbolic importance of sight in the play?

15. Draw up a table showing resemblances between the main plot of Lear and his daughters, and the subplot of Gloucester and his sons.

16. Write down at least three examples of how the play shows the rich and powerful in a critical light.

17. Make notes on how Albany changes during the course of the play.

18. The cuts made in the Folio version of the play include the mock trial of Act III Scene 6 and all of Act IV Scene 3. What is lost if these two episodes are removed and do you think these losses damage the play?

19. Kent and Edgar remain in disguise until the last scene. Make notes on whether it would have been possible for them to reveal their identities earlier. And if so, why do they not do so?

20. How do Edgar's experiences help him gain qualities which may be beneficial to him as a king?

## Section Two: Working towards the exam

Choose one of the following five tasks which require longer, more developed answers. In each case, read the question carefully, select the key areas you need to address, and plan an essay of six to seven points. Write a first draft, giving yourself an hour to do so. Make sure you include supporting evidence for each point, including quotations.

1. '*King Lear* gives us a totally pessimistic picture of the human condition.' Do you agree?
2. Despite its tragic subject, *King Lear* is a gripping, suspenseful work of drama. Choose an extract from the play and analyse how dramatic interest is maintained.
3. In what ways does *King Lear* illustrate the idea that power corrupts?
4. To what extent do you agree that Lear achieves redemption through suffering?
5. A tragic hero is often defined as an important person who suffers a colossal downfall, partly through a flaw in their character, and whose experiences show us the capacities and limits of human life. How well does this definition apply to Lear?

| **Progress check** (rate your understanding on a level of 1 – low, to 5 – high) | 1 | 2 | 3 | 4 | 5 |
|---|---|---|---|---|---|
| The significance of particular events and how they relate to each other | | | | | |
| Why Lear's decision to divide the kingdom affects the lives of all the characters | | | | | |
| How the main plot and the subplot mirror one another | | | | | |
| How some of the characters' actions bring about their own downfall | | | | | |
| Why Edgar becomes the new ruler at the end of the play | | | | | |

## CHARACTERS

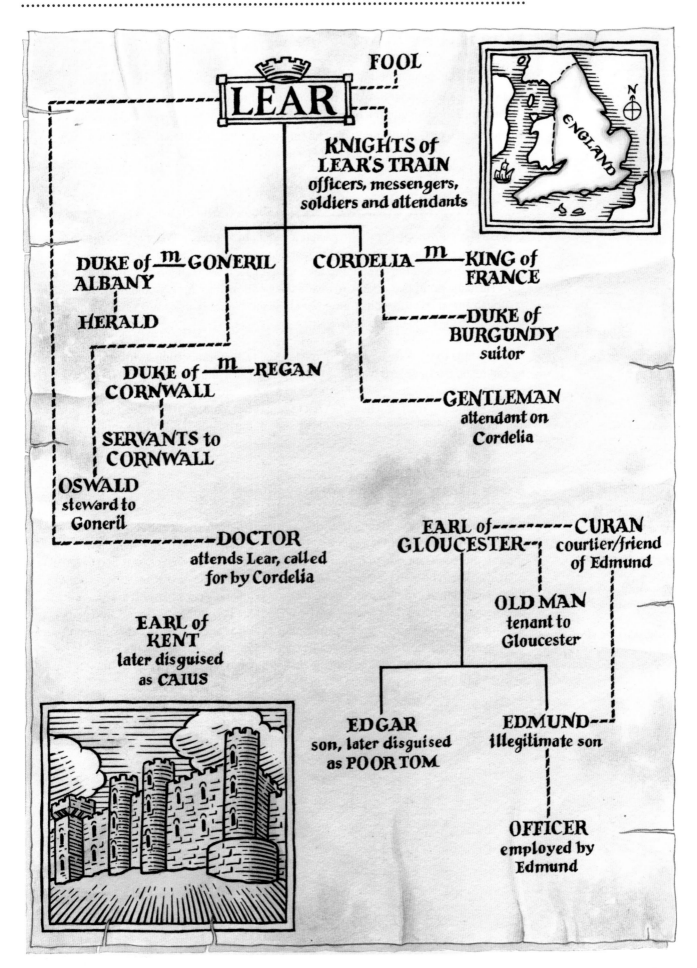

FOOL

LEAR

KNIGHTS of
LEAR'S TRAIN
officers, messengers,
soldiers and attendants

ENGLAND

DUKE of ALBANY — m — GONERIL

CORDELIA — m — KING of FRANCE

HERALD

DUKE of BURGUNDY
suitor

DUKE of CORNWALL — m — REGAN

GENTLEMAN
attendant on
Cordelia

SERVANTS to
CORNWALL

OSWALD
steward to
Goneril

DOCTOR
attends Lear, called
for by Cordelia

EARL of GLOUCESTER — CURAN
courtier/friend
of Edmund

OLD MAN
tenant to
Gloucester

EARL of
KENT
later disguised
as CAIUS

EDGAR
son, later disguised
as POOR TOM

EDMUND
illegitimate son

OFFICER
employed by
Edmund

# KING LEAR

## Who is King Lear?

- Lear is a king of ancient Britain who plans to retire in old age.
- In a moment of anger he exiles his loving daughter Cordelia and his loyal adviser Kent and puts the kingdom into the hands of his two evil daughters.
- Humiliated by Goneril and Regan, he suffers a mental breakdown, but through his 'madness' he begins to see life more clearly.

### An irresponsible character

Lear is a complex **tragic** hero, who excites a variety of responses. Watching his disastrous actions of Act I Scene 1, it is hard not to feel that Lear deserves punishment for his folly. Quick to abusive anger and too arrogant to take advice, Lear is blind and irresponsible as father and ruler. His 'darker purpose' (I.1.35), to divide the kingdom into three, would have alarmed the Jacobean audience, who would remember how the question of the succession had loomed large during the reign of Elizabeth I.

Lear attempts to separate power from responsibility. He is preoccupied with appearances. If he can retain the trappings of majesty without the 'cares and business' of ruling (I.1.38), he is content. It is also possible to see his desire to rely on Cordelia's 'kind nursery' (I.1.123) as selfish. He intends marrying her off in Act I Scene 1 but expects to be nursed while he crawls 'unburdened' (I.1.40) towards death. At the start of the play, Lear is both tyrannical patriarch and demanding child.

### A character who inspires some sympathy

Yet we do sympathise with this egotistical autocrat. In Act II, Lear's better qualities are revealed. His hiring of Kent is a sign that Lear inspires loyalty, and his interaction with the Fool shows a more tolerant side to his nature. It also becomes clear that Lear is trying to remain calm even when he feels he is being wronged (I.4.65–9). In the next scene Lear recognises that he has behaved foolishly and treated Cordelia unkindly (I.5.24). As his insight and troubles grow, so does our concern. We begin to share his outrage as Goneril and Regan become more repugnant. There is desperation as well as egotism in his confrontation with his 'dog-hearted' (IV.3.45) daughters in Act II Scene 4. Gradually Lear's rages become signs of impotence, not authority. By the time he rushes out into the storm our sympathies are likely to lie – and remain – with the beleaguered king.

---

**KEY INTERPRETATION**

The writer Charles Lamb believed the part of King Lear could not be brought fully to life in the theatre, complaining in 1811 that 'an old man tottering about the stage with a walking stick' was inadequate to the great and complex vision that Shakespeare's words created. A similar view has been expressed by some later critics. How well in your experience have actors succeeded in portraying Lear?

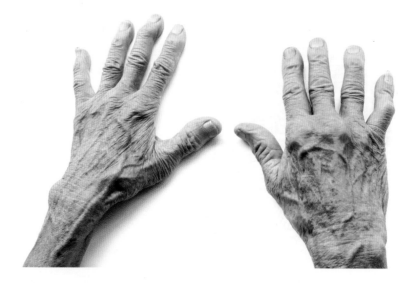

# Study focus: A learning process?

**A02**

Many critics see Lear's breakdown as a learning process. Lear needs to suffer to improve his understanding of himself and the society in which he lives. Certainly he considers a number of topics he had previously paid little attention to: the wretched condition of the poor, the corrupt justice system, true necessity. He learns to distinguish between appearances and reality and considers the sufferings of those close to him. Lear also becomes much more self-critical. He emerges from his torment a more humble, loving and appealing character.

However, other commentators suggest that Lear remains self-obsessed and vengeful. His reflections on the heath are punctuated by thoughts of punishing Goneril and Regan. He struggles to accept responsibility for his elder daughters' cruel natures and never fully acknowledges the folly of his earlier actions. What is your opinion?

**A03** **KEY CONTEXT**

Today, more people are living into old age than ever before. Because of this, it seems likely that a modern audience will be particularly fascinated by Lear's struggle to make sense of his life in his declining years and by the apparent symptoms of dementia with which he seems to struggle in the process.

## Reconciliation

Shakespeare does not allow us to remain too critical of Lear. We see the king in his best light in his reconciliation with Cordelia. Ashamed of his former unkindness, he humbles himself before his youngest daughter. By the end of the play he seems almost to move beyond himself. He has certainly accepted his powerless, diminished status and now sees himself primarily as Cordelia's father. His language reflects his progress. Gone is the royal 'we'. Now Lear uses the first person when he speaks of himself and his feelings. Cordelia is reclaimed lovingly as 'my Cordelia' (V.3.20). In Act V Lear clings to his 'best object' (I.1.213) protectively. He revenges her death by killing the 'slave' responsible for hanging her.

In all of his speeches in Act V Scene 3, the dying king focuses on Cordelia and the overwhelming grief he feels at her passing. Lear's love for and defence of Cordelia go a long way to redeeming him from charges of egotism. He has clearly learned the value of true emotion. His recognition of the injustice of Cordelia's death suggests that his judgement has been restored (V.3.306–7). But wisdom comes too late. Watching the final bleak moments of the play, it is easy to feel that Lear's sufferings have been in vain.

## Key quotation: King Lear

**A01**

Exposed to the storm in Act III, Lear's feelings of abandonment and vulnerability lead him to sympathise with the poor and outcast, and to feel anger at powerful people who exploit others. At first he tries to exempt himself, claiming 'I am a man / More sinned against than sinning' (III.2.59–60). But as his mind struggles to come to terms with his loss of privilege and the insights that his new situation gives him, he is forced to admit that as a ruler he has failed in his responsibility to the most vulnerable (III.4.32–3). While Lear's suffering may be terrible, we see here that it also has some benefit in breaking down his self-centred view of life so that he is able to start to feel humility and compassion.

## Further key quotations

- Goneril assesses Lear's banishment of Cordelia and Kent: 'You see how full of changes his age is.' (I.1.287).
- Lear questions his reduced status: 'Who is it that can tell me who I am?' (I.4.228).
- Lear's self-assessment to Cordelia: 'I am a very foolish fond old man, / Fourscore and upward, not an hour more or less; / And, to deal plainly, I fear I am not in my perfect mind.' (IV.7.60–3).

# GONERIL AND REGAN

## Who are Goneril and Regan?

- Goneril and Regan are Lear's elder daughters, between whom he divides control of Britain when he retires.
- Regan is married to the ruthless Duke of Cornwall, Goneril to the loyal Duke of Albany.
- They unite to take Lear's remaining power and to fight Cordelia's forces, yet are themselves mortal rivals for the love of Edmund.
- Eventually, Regan poisons Goneril and, when challenged over her actions, stabs herself to death.

### Equally evil

Initially, Goneril seems to be the dominant sister. She decides that something must be done to ensure that Lear's rough treatment of Cordelia does not extend to Regan and herself. It is also Goneril who raises the issue of Lear's knights and provokes the first confrontation with her father in Act I Scene 4. Up to this point Regan seems happy to follow Goneril's course of action. But we get hints of her particular brand of sadism in Act I Scene 2 when she urges Cornwall to inflict further punishment on Kent. And then in Act II Scene 4 she leads the onslaught against Lear. The sisters are now vicious equals. Both participate in what is for many the most horrific scene in the play, the blinding of Gloucester. Goneril suggests the method of torture, 'Pluck out his … eyes!' (III.7.55), and then Regan assaults Gloucester, tearing a hair from his beard, and egging her husband on to further cruelty.

## Study focus: Subversive figures **A02**

Lear's elder daughters can be seen as subversive figures who share many character traits. Both are threatening and autocratic, cold and ambitious. Both lust after Edmund in a predatory and unfeminine way. They are masculine in other ways, too. Goneril denies Albany's authority as well as traditional morality, arrogantly asserting her own power when she says, 'the laws are mine, not thine' (V.3.158). Regan may not be an adulteress, but she is a murderess, like her sister. She does 'man's work' when she runs the servant through with a sword in Act III Scene 7.

Goneril and Regan's vindictive assertiveness would have been particularly shocking to a Jacobean audience. Renaissance models of femininity required women to be quiet and submissive. Among Lear's highest praise for Cordelia is that her voice was 'soft, / Gentle and low, an excellent thing in woman' (V.3.272–3), but his elder daughters subvert all the accepted codes of feminine behaviour. They set out to destroy the family and the state. They are agents of chaos and misrule. The terror the sisters inspire is emphasised by the animal **imagery** in the play and by the abhorrence of female sexuality exhibited, especially by Lear.

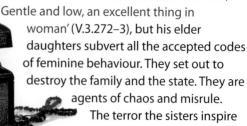

### Remorseless and inhumane

Is it possible to construct a feminist defence of Goneril and Regan? We might recognise the validity of their complaints about Lear in Act I Scene 1; we might sympathise with them because they are not Lear's favourites; we might reflect that they have been constrained by limiting ideas about womanhood and in reaction assert themselves with courage and ambition. Nonetheless, we still have to abhor them as evil. Even Edmund comments on their bad natures. Jealous, treacherous, immoral – these two display all the most distressing features of inhumanity, murdering and maiming without remorse.

The best that can be said for Goneril and Regan is that they are energetic in their pursuit of self-gratification. Ultimately we are obliged to reject Goneril and Regan utterly, even if there is a horrible fascination in watching them at work.

## Key quotation: Goneril and Regan **A01**

Upon discovering Albany's reluctance to fight against Lear and Cordelia, and his horror at the way that Gloucester has been treated, Goneril tells Edmund, 'I must change arms at home, and give the distaff / Into my husband's hands' (IV.2.17-8).

Goneril is not only rejecting the role of obedient wife, but is seeking to reverse normal gender expectations. Her husband is fit only for domestic duties, symbolised by the 'distaff' (a stick used in the spinning of wool). She will 'change arms' and take on his position as a military leader, becoming the bearer of the sword. The Folio version of the text reads 'change names', which carries the equivalent meaning that Albany will in future be known as the wife and she as the husband. Her plan thereafter is to dispose of Albany and replace him with the more congenial Edmund. Regan is happier with her husband Cornwall, whose ambition and viciously violent temper clearly suit her outlook, but his death in Act III Scene 7 leaves her free to pursue Edmund too.

## Further key quotations

- Cordelia on her sisters' hypocritical flattery: 'I shall never marry like my sisters, / To love my father all' (I.1.102–3).
- Goneril invites Regan to co-operate against their father: 'Pray you, let us hit together' (I.1.302–3).
- Lear on the pain his daughters cause him: 'How sharper than a serpent's tooth it is / To have a thankless child!' (I.4.287–8).
- Lear characterises Goneril and Regan: 'Unnatural hags' (II.4.277).
- Albany on the two sisters' treatment of Lear: 'Tigers, not daughters' (IV.2.40).
- Edmund sees the danger of their rivalry over his love: 'Each jealous of the other, as the stung / Are of the adder' (V.1.56–7).

## Revision task 6: The depiction of women **A05**

'The play offers us only simple female stereotypes: the saintly Cordelia and her two wicked sisters.'

Do you agree with this assessment? Makes notes for and against the above proposition. Then write a concluding paragraph, summarising your own view.

**A03**   **KEY CONNECTION**

The film based on Jane Smiley's novel *A Thousand Acres* (1997) updates the Lear story to a large farm in Iowa. Told through the point of view of Ginny, who is a sympathetic equivalent of Goneril, the film offers a viewpoint that the play does not allow us, offering a unique, anti-patriarchal perspective on the characters of Lear and Cordelia.

**A03**   **KEY CONNECTION**

When Ian McKellen played Lear, he was so struck by the contrast between Cordelia and her sisters Regan and Goneril that he wore two wedding rings, implying that they were the offspring of different marriages. However, at IV.3.32–5, Kent states that Lear had all his children by the same wife.

# CORDELIA

## Who is Cordelia?

- Cordelia is Lear's youngest daughter. Although she is his favourite, she refuses to take part in his love-test and he banishes her.
- Having married the King of France, she returns to Britain with a French army to combat her evil sisters and restore Lear's fortunes.
- She loses the battle and is hanged on Edmund's order.

### A problematic heroine

Lear's favourite daughter is possibly more problematic for audiences today than she would have been for the Jacobean theatregoer. She can seem infuriatingly pious. Why does she refuse to take part in Lear's love-test, when she knows how evil Goneril and Regan are? Can we blame her for the violence and cruelty of her sisters' reign? And what of Cordelia's public subversion of Lear's authority, humiliating him in front of the court? These are awkward questions.

Some critics interpret her refusal to speak flattering words to Lear and her acceptance of France as acts of defiance; she is in direct conflict with patriarchy on both occasions, refusing to submit to her father's will. Her stubborn 'Nothing' (I.1.86) leads the way for Goneril and Regan's rebellion. If we follow these arguments through, it is possible to interpret Cordelia's death as a reward for her early disobedience. These, however, are extreme views, which do not really fit in with the portrayal of Cordelia's character in Acts IV and V, or with the consistently high esteem in which Cordelia is held by the 'good' characters. Remember, France takes her for her virtues alone.

## Study focus: Cordelia's virtues **A02**

It is necessary to look at Cordelia's motives in Act I Scene 1. She is seeking to alert Lear to his poor judgement. Her refusal to participate in a glib public-speaking contest can be seen as a sign of her integrity. As the play progresses we learn to distrust all the characters who have an easy way with words. Cordelia's 'Nothing' (I.1.86) looks increasingly honest and worthy.

When she returns in Act IV Cordelia is anything but subversive. In the Quarto version of the play we are prepared for her reappearance by Kent and the Gentleman, who stress her feminine beauty and modesty and the pain she feels when hearing about Lear's sufferings. We are presented with a perfect daughter who will act as redeemer. In Act IV Scene 7 she is solicitous and respectful towards her father, restored as Lear's 'best object' (I.1.213). It is probably this Cordelia we remember: the selfless daughter, full of pity and love.

**A02**

# Progress booster: The significance of Cordelia's death

Cordelia's death has troubled critics and audiences since the play was first performed, and various explanations have been put forward as to why it occurs. Be aware of these explanations and consider which of them you find most convincing.

When Lear carries on Cordelia's corpse, shouting in agony, we are appalled. Like Lear we want to know why 'a dog, a horse, a rat have life, / And thou no breath at all?' (V.3.306–7). It can be argued that an ending in which Britain was taken over by the wife of the French king would have offended the patriotic feelings of Shakespeare's audience and also suggested to them worrying possibilities of future conflict. However, there are also ways of explaining her murder in terms of the play's themes. Shakespeare needs a final cruel blow to bring about Lear's death. Perhaps Cordelia's death is an expression of the playwright's tragic vision. It might also be a final example of man's inhumanity to man in the world of *King Lear*. Shakespeare perhaps wants to show the full horror of the consequences of Lear's folly. For some, Cordelia's death is the real **tragedy** of *King Lear*.

## The final evaluation

Our assessment of Cordelia should probably conclude that although she is as stubborn as the rest of her family, she is a paragon in comparison with her sisters. In two telling lines Lear says 'Her voice was ever soft / Gentle and low – an excellent thing in a woman' (V.3.272–3). It is impossible to imagine Lear's other two 'dog-hearted' (IV.3.45) daughters ever being described in this way. Cordelia's characterisation goes some way to counteract the vicious, masculine cruelty of Goneril and Regan, and the abhorrence of the female that is so prevalent in the play. Shakespeare clearly intends us to agree that hers is a death worth avenging.

**A05 KEY INTERPRETATION**

Feminist critics such as Valerie Traub have complained that the feisty Cordelia of Act I is later replaced by a figure who offers 'a complete capitulation' to sexist norms, subservient and forgiving to the father who had rejected her. Would you agree that, to bring the play to a conclusion, Shakespeare closes off the subversive perspectives he had earlier shown us, or do you think that Cordelia's change of attitude towards Lear is an understandable response to their changed relationship?

## Key quotation: Cordelia's merits  **A01**

The Earl of Kent gives his support to Cordelia: 'The Gods to their dear shelter take thee, maid, / That justly think'st and hast most rightly said!' (I.1.181–2).

Without this intervention we might interpret Cordelia's refusal to flatter Lear in the love-test as ungracious and confrontational. Kent reassures us that one of the most senior figures at court shares Cordelia's disgust at Lear's actions and shares also her belief that it is time for plain talking. Lear, in his self-regard, thinks that rejecting Cordelia and banishing Kent is the next best thing to destroying them, but Kent foresees that someone with Cordelia's merits will always be able to find 'dear shelter' elsewhere.

## Further key quotations

- Lear's plan for Cordelia in the love-test: 'I loved her most, and thought to set my rest / On her kind nursery' (I.1.122–3).
- The King of France values Cordelia despite Lear's rejection of her, calling her 'this unprized precious maid' (I.1.258).
- Praise from a Gentleman for Cordelia's self-control: 'it seemed she was a queen / Over her passion; who, most rebel-like, / Sought to be king o'er her' (IV.3.13–5).

# GLOUCESTER

## Who is Gloucester?

- The Earl of Gloucester is a leading figure at court, whose illegitimate son Edmund convinces him that his loyal elder son Edgar intends to kill him.

- When Lear's life is threatened, Gloucester arranges his escape, but Cornwall blinds Gloucester in punishment.

- The disguised Edgar guides his blind father, helping him work through his suicidal feelings. When Edgar reveals his true identity, Gloucester is overcome by emotion and dies.

## Study focus: Parallels with the king

It is important to note that while Gloucester has some individual features – his superstition, his adultery, for example – his character is determined largely by the parallel role he plays to the king. He is a **foil** to Lear, emphasising features which they have in common. Like Lear, he is a complacent father, used to assuming an unquestioned authority. Like Lear, Gloucester acts rashly and ruthlessly when he believes that his son Edgar has rebelled against him, and in so doing puts himself in his evil son's power. Like Lear, Gloucester fails to 'keep his house in order'. His adultery, which he jokes about in the opening moments of the play, might be seen as a failure to take his patriarchal responsibilities seriously. He is as blind as his ruler and, like him, consequently suffers a tragic fall.

In shadowing Lear's folly so closely, Gloucester perhaps suggests to us that the king's behaviour is not totally abnormal, but what we might expect from someone who has had authority so long that they have come to take their superiority for granted. Set in their ways, sure of themselves and used to being deferred to by those around them, Gloucester and Lear are complacent about the wisdom of their decisions and desperately unaware of their own vulnerability.

## Gloucester's qualities

For much of Act II Gloucester seems to lack resolution. He tries vainly to keep the peace between Lear and his daughters; it is difficult not to judge him harshly when his doors are shut against the king. Faced by the new rulers and their ruthless orders, all he can offer are faint-hearted protests (II.4.299–301). Where Lear responds to **tragedy** with a range of emotions, including raging at the elements, Gloucester is more straightforwardly downcast and suicidal.

Gloucester also displays more positive qualities, however. When he takes action he is brave and determined. He helps Lear on the heath, providing a litter to transport him to safety. Gloucester is heroic in Act III Scene 7, denouncing Goneril and Regan ferociously. He proves that he can be stoical in the face of monstrous cruelty: 'I am tied to th'stake, and I must stand the course' (III.7.53).

When he learns the truth about Edmund, Gloucester's tormented desire to be reconciled with Edgar redeems him. Like Lear, Gloucester becomes increasingly generous as he suffers. He expresses great pity for Lear in Act IV and is genuinely concerned about the dangers the old man and Poor Tom face when helping him. His developing concern for social justice mirrors that of Lear.

### More sinned against than sinning?

To some extent, Gloucester's pain and despair reflect Lear's. While the king raves about his daughters, Gloucester confesses sadly that he is 'almost mad' (III.4.167) himself, thinking about Edgar's supposed treachery. Even after his 'fall' at Dover cliff and his agreement to 'bear / Affliction till it do cry out itself / "Enough, enough", and die' (IV.6.75–7), Gloucester remains suicidal. He welcomes Oswald's threat to kill him and is still deeply depressed as late as Act V Scene 2. His dark thoughts play a key role in establishing and maintaining the bleak atmosphere of the second half of the play. His willingness to die perhaps points towards the carnage of Act V Scene 3, preparing us for the final **tragic** outcome.

Gloucester's death can be seen as a 'dry run' for Lear's. Some critics see Lear's passing as a mirror image of Gloucester's. The old earl dies when his 'flawed heart – / Alack, too weak the conflict to support – / 'Twixt two extremes of passion, joy and grief, / Burst smilingly' (V.3.196–9). The reconciliation with Edgar is too much for him to bear.

Gloucester is punished very harshly for his misjudgements of character. Edgar's verdict, that he dies for adultery, is not easily accepted. For all his faults, Gloucester will probably be viewed by most audiences as a character more sinned against than sinning.

**A01** **PROGRESS BOOSTER**

Shakespeare is not generally considered a realistic writer, so when writing about his characterisation it is not appropriate to speculate at length about his characters' inner motives and psychology. Examiners will be much more impressed if you focus on the details of how the characters are conveyed through the drama and how they contribute to its development.

## Key quotation: Gloucester's vision  **A01**

After he has been blinded, Gloucester tells the old man who is leading him, 'I stumbled when I saw' (IV.1.19). When he had the sense of sight, he failed to see the truth that Edgar loved him and Edmund was a lying schemer. Now he has been blinded, and seemingly lost everything, he has at least gained in understanding.

## Further key quotations

- Edmund's dismissive summary: 'A credulous father' (I.2.183)
- Gloucester shows his courage: 'If I die for it, as no less is threatened me, the King, my old master, must be relieved' (III.3.17–9).
- Gloucester prepares to kill himself, but thinks of Edgar: 'If Edgar live, O, bless him!' (IV.6.40).

# EDGAR

## Who is Edgar?

- Edgar is the Earl of Gloucester's oldest son, accused by his brother Edmund of wanting to murder their father. He escapes pursuit by disguising himself as a mentally-disturbed beggar, Poor Tom.

- Using various identities, Edgar looks after his father once the latter has been blinded. He dissuades him from suicide and saves him from murder, finding as he does so incriminating evidence about Edmund.

- Ultimately, Edgar kills his brother Edmund and, after Lear has died, he becomes the British king.

## A mere plot device?

Many critics feel dissatisfied with Edgar. He plays so many roles and performs such a wide range of functions; is he simply a plot device? Shakespeare does not spend much time establishing Edgar's virtues before having him disguise himself as Poor Tom. Gloucester's legitimate son starts the play as passive and easily deceived by Edmund. In Act I he shows none of the heroism he displays later in the play. So how are we to view his lightning changes?

It is possible to detect progression in Edgar's characterisation as he moves from one role to another. He grows in stature through his use of disguises. He is forced to assume the garb of a 'madman' to preserve his life, but his final disguise – masked avenger – enables him to take command of his own fate. Those who complain of Edgar's weak gullibility also forget that Jacobean audiences would have understood that good characters were easy to fool. Villains were accepted as being so cunning that their evil intentions were impossible to detect. Edgar's willingness to be guided by Edmund might be seen as proof of his worthiness.

# Study focus: A player of roles

On the heath, the role of Poor Tom pushes Edgar centre stage. Many critics have noticed how the presence of the feigned 'madman' helps Lear. As Poor Tom, Edgar is a companion willing to follow the wild sequence of Lear's thoughts and enter into the fantasies through which Lear expresses his emotions. As he interacts with Poor Tom, Lear's humanity and understanding increase.

Edgar also comments on Lear and Gloucester's suffering, guiding audience responses to the two patriarchs in Acts III and IV. He is actively generous, too. In Act IV Edgar guides Gloucester and tries to chase away his gloomy thoughts ('Why I do trifle thus with his despair / Is done to cure it', IV.6.33–4). Like Cordelia, Edgar feels sympathy for the father who rejected him so brutally.

Notice, too, that at the end of Act IV Scene 6, Edgar's role-playing enables him to defend Gloucester when Oswald threatens him. To preserve Edgar's moral character (revengers in Jacobean drama often have sinister motives), Shakespeare shows us his remorse: 'I am only sorry / He had no other deathsman' (IV.6.254–5). His courage and spirit awakened, Edgar is now ready to challenge Edmund. His facility with language has been used to protect himself and others and we could argue that his deceptions are essentially honest.

**KEY INTERPRETATION** **A05**

In his study *Poor Tom* (2014), Simon Palfrey endeavours to make a case that Edgar's role-play turns him into 'one of the most expressive figures Shakespeare ever created … a figure without conventional limits'. Palfrey suggests that Edgar's ability to constantly assume new identities and confront painful experiences gives him an affinity with Shakespeare himself, creator of so many characters and explorer of their deepest feelings. Do you find this view of Edgar convincing?

## An agent of justice

In Act V Edgar becomes an agent of justice. He helps to restore the old order. It is possible to view Edgar as the only character unsullied enough to rule after Lear's death. He has committed no crime against his family or the state. He has never questioned the authority of his elders. He took action when necessary. The worst we can accuse Edgar of is leaving it very late to reveal himself to Gloucester, and he is heartily sorry for this, breaking off from his account of his father's death to exclaim, 'O fault!' (V.3.192).

Edgar has endured appalling privation and has managed to show mercy and strength. When he speaks of his journey through the play as a 'pilgrimage' (V.3.196) we understand the serious sense of purpose behind Edgar's role-playing. Surely he has proved himself many times over? When he unassumingly takes charge ('The weight of this sad time we must obey', V.3.323), we have some justification for feeling that his succession is an appropriate conclusion.

## A less sympathetic figure

In the climactic Act V, Edgar's uncompromising judgement of his father's 'crimes' appears disturbing: 'The dark and vicious place where thee he got / Cost him his eyes' (V.3.172–3). What has happened to Edgar's sense of pity? Previously he had greeted his blinded father with the tender cry, 'Bless thy sweet eyes' (IV.1.53). His desire to put his brother in his place seems for a time to have driven away more positive feelings. Moreover, his declaration that the gods are just looks decidedly suspect when Cordelia dies.

## Key quotation: Edgar's roles  **A01**

When Edgar adopts his disguise as Poor Tom, he tells himself, 'Edgar I nothing am' (II.3.21). His words seem to imply that, by adopting a false identity, he will lose touch with his real one completely.

The word 'nothing' occurs throughout the play as characters lose what they held dear and face oblivion. Yet as the play progresses, Edgar become more at ease with the role-switching to which he has had to resort. Edgar is able to make good use of his false identities and to re-emerge as himself whenever he wishes, but it is as a renewed self who has gained valuable experience and skills from the part he has played.

**A05**  KEY INTERPRETATION

In Adrian Noble's 1993 Royal Shakespeare Company performance, Edgar became a figure of vengeance who has been so traumatised by the blinding of his father that he pokes out Oswald's eyes before killing him and tries to gouge out Edmund's eyes with his thumbs during their fight. Does this interpretation of Edgar as emotionally disturbed help explain his determination as a fighter, or does it diminish him?

**A02**  KEY INTERPRETATION

In comparison with the titanic Lear, who faces his suffering head on in full view of the audience, Edgar can seem a less perceptive, more limited figure. Although it is possible to argue that he is the most creative character in the play, in practice Edgar tends to appear on stage for brief periods at a time in a variety of guises, usually keeping his deepest feelings hidden, and this restricts his impact. In the end our reception of his character depends heavily upon how he is played. Edgar's heroic qualities can be stressed, and in performance his disparate parts can be forged into a more or less satisfactory whole.

## EDMUND

### Who is Edmund?

- Edmund is the illegitimate son of the Earl of Gloucester. By convincing his father that his older son Edgar is plotting against him, he is able to replace Edgar as Gloucester's heir.

- Edmund betrays Gloucester to Regan, Goneril and their husbands. They blind the earl and give his title to Edmund, whom Goneril and Regan both desire and who therefore sees an opportunity to become king.

- Edmund is arrested for treason by Goneril's husband, Albany, and killed in a fight with Edgar, but not before he has arranged for the murder of Lear and Cordelia.

### A Machiavellian villain

Like many villains in Jacobean drama, Edmund seethes with frustration about the 'plague of custom' (I.2.3) that keeps him on the fringes of society, in this case his illegitimacy. His **Machiavellian** qualities include his political ambition and willingness to use unscrupulous methods to achieve his aims.

Initially we may sympathise with him when we hear the coarse way that Gloucester jokes about his conception. Edmund and his mother are spoken of with such disrespect that he will clearly not be able to achieve the status he desires if he sticks to normal methods. As Edmund says himself, he is adaptable and ready to manipulate events to serve his turn: 'all with me's meet / that I can fashion fit' (I.2.188). His ability to adopt the right tone in any situation helps him in his progress towards power.

**KEY INTERPRETATION** A05

In many film and TV productions Edmund is shot in close-up, delivering his **soliloquies** directly to camera. Thus, viewers are encouraged to see how seductive and persuasive the villain can be. In the theatre he can step to the front of the stage and speak directly to the audience. How might this presentation differ in its effect?

## Study focus: Not a revolutionary?

Ask yourself whether Edmund really sets himself up against the society he operates in, as some critics suggest. Certainly he sneers at its values, as his toying with the words 'base' and 'legitimate' shows (see I.2.10 and I.2.18–19). Edmund seems to subscribe to a savage code: survival of the fittest. His goddess, Nature, is a brutal, anarchic force, as opposed to the kind aspects of human nature which Gloucester has in mind when he calls him a 'natural boy' (II.1.83).

Edmund never apologises for his wickedness; he revels in it right up to the final scene. All the beliefs he outlines in Act I Scene 2 suggest he rejects the hierarchy that has made his father and brother so prosperous. But his own ambitions are worldly; really, he wants to succeed in society's terms. He aims first at Edgar's inheritance, then at Gloucester's title and finally at the throne of England. He wants to rise up the hierarchy rather than overthrow it. He may be a rebel but he is no revolutionary. Surely Edmund cannot therefore be viewed as an anti-establishment figure?

## Formidably destructive

Yet Edmund is subversive, showing the old order of Lear and Gloucester to be complacent and lacking in vigilance. The speed of his rise, and the eagerness with which he pursues it, are an indication of this. In the cruel world of Goneril and Regan's regime, he fits in very well. He is responsible for the deaths of three princesses, as well as the cruel maiming of his father. His progress is halted too late to save Lear. By the end of the final scene Edmund has proved himself to be formidably destructive. He almost obtains everything he wants.

## Edmund's fall

In the end we come to loathe everything Edmund stands for. We may admire his tenacity and quick wits, enjoy his energetic acting out of roles and the way he takes us into his confidence through his use of **soliloquies**; but in the end we must reject him, as we reject Goneril and Regan. In Act V Scene 3 Edmund is defeated when Albany and Edgar reassert the values of the old order. Now Edmund is forced to reject his own rebel code and submit. His fall is as meteoric as his rise. We know his subversion has failed when we hear him say he will forgive his 'deathsman' if he is of noble blood. His dying desire to do good also seems to cancel out his earlier delight in his own villainy.

Edmund's strange last line, 'Yet Edmund was beloved' (V.3.239), suggests his real motivation all along may have been to overcome a sense of insecurity and emotional exclusion. It could also be read as a confirmation of the virtuous characters' insistence throughout the play that caring and loyalty are important. Even so, despite initial sympathy and admiration for his heroic ambition, few will regret the defiant bastard son's demise.

### Key quotation: Edmund the underdog? **A01**

Edmund ends his first soliloquy with a rousing cry: 'I grow, I prosper; / Now, gods, stand up for bastards!' (I.2.21–2). He has taken the audience into his confidence, speaking his thoughts aloud, and it is likely that at this stage his outlandish words will be greeted with sympathy and even some cheering. We can all appreciate what it is to be undervalued and admire someone who asserts themselves against the odds. However, as we see the methods Edmund employs to pursue success, 'framing' his brother and betraying his father to torture and mutilation, as well as casually undertaking adultery and murder, our sympathy rapidly ebbs away.

**A05** KEY INTERPRETATION

Just as Cordelia's loving acceptance of her father in Act IV can be considered a betrayal of her defiance of him in Act I, so Edmund's acceptance of Edgar's royal nobility seems to undermine his earlier heartfelt criticisms of society as an unjust hierarchy. Do you feel that these changes of heart weaken the play in any way?

**A05** KEY INTERPRETATION

Critic Finian O'Toole suggests that Edgar's defeat of Edmund is a moral triumph which we might reasonably expect to bring the play to a conclusion. Instead, 'we are suddenly faced with this old man who comes back on stage, literally howling'. In his view, this second ending must have been included because Shakespeare wanted to leave us with a sense of life's intractable injustice.

# THE FOOL

## Who is the Fool?

- The Fool is a court jester who entertains Lear with jokes, riddles and songs.
- His witty patter challenges Lear to face up to the terrible error he made in dismissing Cordelia and handing over power to Regan and Goneril.
- The Fool entertains the audience and offers a sharp commentary on characters and events. He provides comic relief from the tragic series of events unfolding.

### A number of roles

The Fool plays a number of roles: voice of conscience, social commentator, truth-teller, representative of Cordelia, vehicle for **pathos**, Lear's alter-ego, dramatic **chorus**. His songs, riddles and epigrams also provide comic relief. The flippant remark about Poor Tom's clothing is a good example of the Fool lightening the tone of a distressing scene (III.4.66). Many of the Fool's other speeches can also be played for comic effect, but it is possible to stress the 'bitter' rather than the witty fool. When he first appears in the play the Fool is extremely critical of Lear: 'Dost thou call me fool, boy?' / 'All thy other titles thou hast given away; that thou wast born with' (I.4.146–8). These lines are typical of the Fool's interaction with Lear. His sarcasm is blunt and hard hitting.

The Fool's bitterness can partly be understood by considering his role as Cordelia's representative. A truth-teller, like Lear's youngest daughter, he pines away when she goes to France. Many of the Fool's early cutting speeches are designed to alert Lear to his daughters' true characters. However, unlike Cordelia, the Fool is never punished for his truth-telling. He is 'all-licensed' (I.4.199), meaning that he is able to say aloud whatever he thinks. Jesters were often kept by the monarch to provide witty analysis of contemporary behaviour and to remind the sovereign of his humanity. Certainly Lear's Fool fulfils these functions for his master.

The Fool also enjoys a close and affectionate relationship with 'nuncle' Lear (II.4.120). It is the Fool Lear calls out to when he fears he is losing his reason. On the heath the king considers his servant's sufferings alongside his own. In return the Fool remains steadfastly loyal. In a play where family relationships are disastrously dysfunctional, the Fool seems to play the role of good son.

The Fool's role as social commentator has been linked to the prophecy he makes at the end of Act III Scene 2. In this speech he comments on the injustices and corruption of Lear's reign (III.2.80–95) and perhaps predicts a better time to come. Throughout the play he draws attention to the chaos Lear has caused in the kingdom by putting his evil daughters in control. The implication of many of his speeches is that Lear has wronged the country as well as himself.

## Study focus: Why does the Fool disappear?

Some critics wonder whether the Fool's relentless criticism drives Lear to despair. Most prefer to believe that the Fool serves a positive function when he criticises his master. He pushes Lear towards the truth and then tries to 'out-jest' his injuries, supporting the king as he makes his terrible journey through Act III. So why does the Fool disappear?

Some commentators suggest Jacobean audiences would not have been disconcerted by the disappearance of a character half way through the play. Other critics think that the Fool is dropped when he is no longer needed. The Fool's role was to help Lear see more clearly and when his job is completed, he vanishes. Other critics suggest it would be inappropriate to have a comic character (however dark his humour) in the bleak final Acts of the play. Finally, it is possible that the same actor played the Fool and Cordelia, reinforcing their similarity as challengers of Lear's conscience, and therefore they could not be on stage at the same time. How do you appraise the role of the Fool?

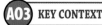

**KEY CONTEXT**

Shakespeare wrote *King Lear* for his drama company, the King's Men, and would have had specific actors in mind for most of the parts. The Fool is likely to have been created as a vehicle for the troupe's comedy actor Robert Armin, whose skills included singing and delivering witty banter.

## Progress booster: Playing the Fool

It is clear from the Fool's references to his motley (I.4.144) and coxcomb (I.4.94) that he wears the traditional costume of a coat of green and yellow, and a hood with ears. Such an outfit was no longer current in Shakespeare's day, which would avoid any embarrassing resemblance between Lear's fool and James I's court jester, Archie Armstrong.

Over the last hundred years, the interpretation and presentation of the Fool have become increasingly important to critics and directors, but also increasingly varied as the tradition of the jester has long since died out. The Fool has been played by women (though not always as female), as a music hall clown, as a waif in ragged clothes, as a worn-out old man, as a young drag queen. In each case, the director seems to be choosing to emphasise a particular aspect of the relationship between Lear and his Fool, and something of his or her vision of the world of *King Lear*. Which version of the Fool do you feel might add most to your understanding of King Lear, the man, and *King Lear*, the play?

## Key quotation: The Fool

The Fool tells Lear, 'I am better than thou art now: I am a Fool; thou art nothing' (I.4.191–2). This assessment of how Lear has undermined his own identity, blunt to the point of cruelty, is delivered when the Fool sees Lear worrying about Goneril's frown. It seems that the Fool is distressed to see the once powerful king reduced to fretting over what mood his daughter may be in. It is a further reflection on Lear's loss of power that he does not answer the Fool back himself. Instead, it is Goneril who delivers a silent rebuke, using another of her frowns ('frontlets').

# KENT

## Who is Kent?

● The Earl of Kent is a leading figure at court, who tries to dissuade Lear from rejecting Cordelia and entrusting the country to Goneril and Regan.

● Exiled by Lear, Kent returns to serve him in disguise, using the name Caius.

● After Lear dies, Kent declines to help run the country, saying that he will soon join his master in death.

### Loyalty and bluntness

Kent's most notable characteristics are loyalty and bluntness. The former motivates him, the latter causes him trouble. Kent speaks up when he sees Lear acting foolishly. He resorts to blunt language – 'What wouldst thou do, old man?' (I.1.145) – only when more respectful interjections are ignored. Thereafter he reverts to addressing Lear as 'my lord' and 'my liege'. His determination to stick to the 'old language' of Lear's court can be seen as a measure of his loyalty. It might also indicate that Kent is a conservative, backward-looking figure. There is other evidence that points in this direction. During Lear's 'madness' Kent is reluctant to allow Poor Tom to accompany his master. Kent is a representative of the hierarchy that Lear destroyed when he gave away his power. It does not come as a surprise to hear him say he expects to die, in Act V Scene 3. The world has moved on and Kent has no place in it now.

---

## Study focus: A positive figure?

Many critics suggest that Kent is a wholly positive figure and there is evidence to support this. His judgement in Act I Scene 1 is sound. Kent accepts banishment but immediately assumes a disguise so that he can continue to follow Lear. He suffers punishment stoically in Act II. Out in the storm he thinks only of his master's comfort. He is constantly active in Lear's service. Although some critics argue that Kent's anger harms Lear's cause, it is a relief to see a character take on Goneril, Regan, Cornwall and Oswald. Kent also keeps us informed about important developments in the plot and acts as Cordelia's champion. Do you support this view of Kent?

---

### Final sorrow

In the second half of the play Kent's tone becomes increasingly melancholy. Does Kent see that he will not be needed for much longer? He comments sorrowfully on his master's passing: 'he hates him / That would upon the rack of this tough world / Stretch him out longer' (V.3.313–15). It is appropriate that the dependable Kent sums up his master's pain in this distressing scene. The world of *King Lear* would be considerably darker without Kent's diligence.

### Key quotation: Kent's loyalty A01

Lear's rejection of Cordelia provokes Kent to interrupt and contradict the king. Kent excuses himself for his behaviour very bluntly: 'Be Kent unmannerly, / When Lear is mad' (I.1.144–5). For Kent loyalty does not mean doing what he is told, but doing what will best support his master, whether his master appreciates it or not.

---

**KEY INTERPRETATION** A05

At the close of the play Kent implies that he is near death: 'I have a journey, sir, shortly to go; / My master calls me, I must not say no' (V.3.321–2). Does Kent mean that he is so drained by the tragedy of his 'master' Lear that his life is now used up, or is he hinting that he will commit suicide rather than live on after him? An actor may be able to indicate which of these applies. In the 2008 film by Trevor Nunn, for example, Jonathan Hyde suggests suicide by placing a hand meaningfully on his dagger.

# ALBANY AND CORNWALL

## Who are Albany and Cornwall?

- Each duke is married to one of Lear's daughters, Albany to Goneril, and Cornwall to Regan.
- Cornwall supports Regan's ruthless greed for power, to the extent of torturing and blinding Gloucester, an atrocity which leads to one of his own servants killing him.
- Albany, in contrast, turns against Goneril and plays a major part in restoring order.

### Albany's initial weakness

Albany makes little impression at first. The audience is suspicious of Goneril long before her husband recognises her inhumanity, and his interjections in the first scene in which he plays any significant part (Act I Scene 4) seem weak. Admittedly, he has missed much of Goneril's hectoring of Lear, but 'What's the matter, Sir?' (I.4.294) is surely inadequate. Are we to assume that Albany is so good himself that he has been taken in by Goneril?

After Lear takes himself off in high dudgeon, Albany wants to wait and see what happens. At this stage he certainly lacks Goneril's force and decisiveness. It is easy to be critical of Albany's inaction and lack of foresight, but they are both necessary to the **plot**. If he attempted to check his wife's progress now, it would distract from the main business of the play at this point – Lear's deteriorating relationship with his daughters.

## Study focus: Contrasting characters **A02**

Albany's rectitude contrasts neatly with Cornwall's increasing ruthlessness. In Act II Scene 1 we see how Regan's unpleasant husband is drawn to Edmund. This is a sure sign that Cornwall is morally dubious. We also quickly realise that, unlike Albany, Cornwall is ready to assume command and join his wife and sister-in-law in their campaign against Lear. His tone is habitually authoritarian. He conducts the investigation into Kent and Oswald's altercation, and announces Kent's punishment in an angry tone that suggests 'the fiery quality of the Duke' (II.4.90).

In Act III Scene 7 Cornwall's contempt for any authority other than his own is made horribly clear. He aspires to the crown and acts as if he were the law. Cornwall is responsible for the most shocking act of physical violence in *King Lear* – the blinding of Gloucester.

### Cornwall falls, Albany rises

Having demonstrated the depths that humanity can sink to, Shakespeare has no further need of Cornwall. His death at the end of Act III enables Shakespeare to set up the sisters' rivalry for Edmund more effectively. The way Cornwall meets his end is also significant – his own servant turns on him, just as he had turned on his host and his king. This is **poetic justice**.

Cornwall's corruption is counterbalanced by his brother-in-law's actions, not his words. Albany rises to the occasion in Act V Scene 3. He denounces and arrests Edmund, offers to challenge him and then presides over the duel between Gloucester's two sons. After the fight, he continues to play a leadership role. He asks Edgar to tell the story of his existence in hiding, enabling the audience to hear of Gloucester's death. It is also Albany who delivers a stern epitaph for Goneril and Regan. Shakespeare now wants us to see him as an agent of justice and correct morality.

**A05** **KEY INTERPRETATION**

Like Goneril and Regan, Cornwall and Albany seem quite passive and obedient in the opening scene, only later emerging as active characters with their own agendas. However, the first two lines of the play indicate that there is already a serious rivalry between them. How might this be made visible in Act I Scene 1 through their positioning and behaviour?

**A03** **KEY CONTEXT**

In *Macbeth*, which was written around the same time as *Lear*, Shakespeare tried to please King James I by making Banquo, an ancestor of the King's, one of the virtuous characters. Similarly, the Duke of Albany was a title held by King James I until he transferred it to his son Prince Charles, and by making Albany the character who defeats the invaders, arrests Edmund and establishes a new order, Shakespeare is again giving James a positive character to whom he can be linked.

When Lear appears, Albany gracefully resigns the 'absolute power' he has briefly assumed as leader of the British forces. But his virtue is hopeless now. In the final moments of the play, his words seem inadequate again. Albany's brief final lines suggest that language cannot express the distress and pity the characters feel at the end of the play.

### Albany's authority

Edgar's last speech is attributed to Albany in the Quarto, reinforcing his authority. But it remains difficult to believe in Albany. He is so often a bystander. One line in particular seems to undermine his good intentions completely. As Cordelia's body is carried onto the stage he calls out in alarm, 'The Gods defend her!' (V.3.255). We are forced to conclude that Albany is out of his depth in the world of *King Lear*.

> ## Key quotations: Albany and Cornwall · **A01**
>
> - Edmund thinks Albany's conscience is a weakness: 'he's full of alteration / And self-reproving' (V.1.3–4).
> - Gloucester fears Cornwall: 'You know the fiery quality of the Duke' (II.4.90).

# OSWALD

### Who is Oswald?

- Oswald is Goneril's steward, in charge of her household.
- He obeys all Goneril's orders without question, even if this means disrespecting the king or trying to kill the blind, elderly Gloucester.
- He is twice beaten by Kent and, as he tries to murder Gloucester, he is killed by Edgar.

> ## Progress booster: The role of Oswald · **A02**
>
> Make sure you understand that, although Oswald is a minor character, he serves a number of useful functions. His most important role is as Goneril's servant. He carries out orders diligently and faithfully and delivers a number of significant letters that move on the action of the play. He is Goneril's agent in corruption and his bad qualities mirror his mistress's warped nature. Oswald is an insolent, cowardly liar and as self-seeking as the other evil characters. Keen to receive a financial reward, he is only too ready to kill Gloucester in Act IV. His selfish opportunism reflects Goneril's greedy ambition. Oswald also provides a contrast to Kent (the honest plain-speaking servant) and awakens Edgar's valour.

> ## Key quotation: Oswald · **A01**
>
> Kent sums up Oswald as 'one that wouldst be a bawd in way of good service' (II.2.18–9) – in other words, as someone who would try to please their employer by leading them into bad ways (a 'bawd' is one who supplies women for sex, a pimp).

### KEY INTERPRETATION · A05

For his 1975 television version, the director Jonathan Miller had to shorten the play. One cut he made was to remove Oswald's attempt to murder Gloucester and Oswald's ensuing death. How do you think the omission of this episode might alter your response to the play – for example, in your view of Oswald and of Edgar?

# THEMES

## Nothing

### The value of 'nothing'

As he loses everything – his status, his family, his mind – Lear learns the value of Cordelia's 'Nothing, my lord' (I.1.86). Her refusal to participate in the love-test sets off the whole disastrous chain of events. Thereafter, other characters help Lear to come to terms with his 'nothingness', using **imagery** that echoes Cordelia's words. The Fool taunts Lear with the word 'nothing' (I.4.128–30 and I.4.184–6), and later the sight of Poor Tom pushes Lear to ask 'Is man no more than this?' (III.4.104–5). Finally, Lear learns how empty Goneril and Regan's words were and finds he has moved closer to Cordelia's true values: 'I know not what to say,' he murmurs (IV.7.54).

Just as Lear has to come to terms with his 'nothingness', so 'nothing' causes Gloucester trouble in the subplot. Like Goneril and Regan, Edmund uses false words to gain everything. Edmund pretends that his fake letter is 'Nothing, my lord', copying Cordelia's reply in an ironic and alarming way (I.2.31). Gloucester too loses everything, and learns to see more clearly.

## Appearance and reality

### Disguises

Ideas about appearance and reality are often expressed through clothing in *King Lear*, since looks so often prove deceptive. Virtuous characters assume disguises in order to survive, continuing to do good in their new lowly roles. The apparel of Lear's closest companions on the heath – the Fool, Kent and Edgar – is significant. All three are humbly dressed; the Fool in his motley, Kent as a man servant and Edgar in the garb of the social outcast. In spite of their inferior status – signified by their clothing – servants are frequently the source of hope, charity and justice in *King Lear*.

## Study focus: The trappings of majesty  **A02**

Ceremonial garments and the clothing of the court are deeply suspect. They conceal the truth. Lear cannot see beyond the trappings of majesty and assumes his crown makes him 'ague-proof' (IV.6.105). Goneril, Regan and Edmund cover up their depravity with attractive exteriors. When Lear is forced to face reality he decides to remove his kingly garments, 'Off, off, you lendings!' (III.4.110–1). He needs to rid himself of the trappings of majesty so that he can learn. In Act IV we know that Lear has gained wisdom when he says astutely 'furred gowns hide all' (IV.6.163). He has recognised the truth about himself and his daughters. When his sanity is restored, Lear is ready to be put in fresh clothes. He no longer needs his crown of poisonous and bitter weeds, a **symbol** of his jarred senses.

**A01**  PROGRESS BOOSTER

Try to comment, where appropriate, on the expressive rhythm of Shakespeare's language. For example, Lear's grief-stricken cry, 'Never, never, never, never, never!' (V.3.308), is made so powerful because the agony Lear feels at his daughter's death is expressed through a radical shift in metre. In a line of iambic pentameter we expect the stresses to fall mostly on the even syllables, but here they fall entirely on the odd ones. Moreover, the actor has to decide whether, where and for how long to pause within this line, and whether the volume of his voice should increase, fall away or stay level. Whatever decisions he makes should reinforce our sense of Lear struggling with his grief.

**A04**  KEY CONNECTION

**Metaphors** of clothing are used throughout Shakespeare's plays, especially when the dramatist is interested in exploring ideas about appearance and reality. Hamlet, for example, insists that his true thoughts and feelings cannot easily be deduced from his appearance: 'I have that within that passes show, / These but the trappings and the suits of woe' (I.2.85–6).

## Key quotations: Loss and disguises  **A01**

- Lear begins to glimpse his loss: 'nothing can be made out of nothing' (I.4.131).
- Cordelia sees through her sisters' falsehoods: 'Time shall unfold what plighted cunning hides' (I.1.279).
- Edgar warns against vain appearances: 'set not thy sweet heart on proud array' (III.4.83–4).

# Sight and blindness

### Seeing clearly

The importance of seeing yourself and the world clearly is a key theme in *King Lear*. In Act I Scene 1, trying to warn the king that he is behaving foolishly, Kent urges him, 'see better, Lear' (I.1.157). He begs his master to let him remain 'The true blank of thine eye' (I.1.158), but receives an angry dismissal, 'Out of my sight' (I.1.156). However, another critic forces Lear to consider his actions more closely. The Fool sums up Lear's folly neatly with a **metaphor**, 'So out went the candle, and we were left darkling' (I.4.216). This line serves as a prediction for the end of Act II, when Lear is overwhelmed by dark thoughts and shut out in the storm. We might also see Lear as the candle. As monarch he is the source of light and life in the kingdom. When he fails, all the characters associated with Lear are 'left darkling'.

**KEY CONTEXT** **A03**

Gloucester remarks to Edmund, 'if it be nothing, I shall not need spectacles' (I.2.34–5). The use of spectacles was quite common in Renaissance Europe, especially once printed books had become widely available; reading glasses could be bought from peddlers in the street. It is possible that Gloucester's metaphorical lack of perceptiveness might even be **symbolised** by his making use of a pair of spectacles on stage.

### Gloucester's blindness

After the storm, Lear's ability to see more clearly is apparent when he meets Gloucester and tells him, 'A man may see how this world goes with no eyes' (IV.6.148–9). Some critics find Lear's puns about eyes desperately cruel. But Gloucester and Lear do now 'see how the world goes'. They both 'stumbled' when they could see. Gloucester's blinding is the physical manifestation of the mental torture Lear endured on the heath. We are prepared for it by a series of references to sight. In Act I Scene 2 Gloucester asked Edmund to 'look into' Edgar's treachery and then in Act III Scene 7 the references to eyes come thick and fast, starting with Goneril's 'Pluck out his eyes!' (III.7.5).

## Study focus: Lear and Cordelia **A02**

Until Cordelia returns, we feel that all is 'dark and comfortless' (III.7.83). Notice how Cordelia is associated with healing tears and radiant light. Throughout his confrontations with Goneril and Regan, and during his descent into mental instability, Lear refuses to weep: 'Old fond eyes … I'll pluck ye out' he declares vehemently (I.4.300–1). His desperate struggle against weeping can be seen as proof of Lear's determination not to be vanquished by his pelican daughters. However, he cries when he is reunited with Cordelia. Is this a sign of weakness or an indication that he sees himself and his daughter more clearly?

In Act V, Lear is defiant again: he and Cordelia will not weep in prison. When she is hanged, Lear finally gives in to his grief, telling the onlookers, 'Had I your tongues and eyes, I'd use them so / That heaven's vault should crack' (V.3.258–9). His eyes at last fail him as he mourns the loss of his 'best object' (I.1.213).

## Key quotations: Blindness as a metaphor **A01**

- Gloucester sums up the tragic state of the world: ''Tis the times' plague, when madmen lead the blind' (IV.1.46).
- Lear acknowledges his frailty: 'Mine eyes are not o'th'best: I'll tell you straight' (V.3.279).

# Madness

## Different types of madness

Several types of 'madness' feature in *King Lear*. Lear's rash actions of Act I Scene 1 might be viewed as political insanity. The bloodlust exhibited by Goneril, Regan and Cornwall is an abhorrent kind of irrationality. Does the king's descent into mental torment at least cure his moral blindness? If so, the cost is terrible. Lear compares his state of mind to the torments of hell. Once he finally regains his judgement, Lear is tormented again when Cordelia dies. In his final moments he seems deluded anew, believing that his daughter still breathes.

There are other types of 'madness' that shed a sombre light on Lear's mental state: the Fool's professional madness (his clowning), Edgar's feigned madness and Gloucester's half-crazed pity. Yet the Fool's jests often lighten the tone and some of Edgar's antics as Poor Tom are probably intended to amuse – some Elizabethans visited Bedlam (Bethlehem) Hospital to enjoy the spectacle of 'mad' beggars. However, Edgar's suffering also seems designed to heighten the **pathos** of Act III. His descriptions of being driven close to suicide by devils and the mock trial can be very disturbing on stage. Ultimately, the madness of *King Lear* in all its forms is deeply distressing. It develops from and points back to the king's instability.

> ## Key quotation: Fear of madness                      **A01**
>
> ● Lear exclaims, 'O let me not be mad, not mad, sweet heaven!' (I.5.43). His awareness of his own deterioration adds pathos to his position.

**A03** **KEY CONTEXT**

According to the philosopher Aristotle, horror and pity are the predominant emotions that an audience feel when they are watching a **tragedy**. Since madness is a subject particularly likely to arouse such feelings, it is no wonder that madness features prominently in *King Lear*, and in other Shakespearean tragedies such as *Hamlet* and *Macbeth*.

# Suffering

Many of the characters suffer almost beyond endurance, reflected in the **imagery** of the play. Lear tells Regan that her sister has 'struck' (II.4.158) him with her tongue and 'tied / Sharp-tooth'd unkindness' (II.4.132–3) around his heart. His daughters are 'a disease that's in my flesh … a boil / A plague-sore, or embossed carbuncle, / In my corrupted blood' (II.4.221–4). Even when his senses are restored, Lear continues to suffer. He has been 'cut to th' brains' and finds it impossible to recover (IV.6.191). 'Burning shame' keeps him from Cordelia (IV.3.46). Despite their companions' efforts to help, Gloucester dies of a broken heart and Lear's moment of greatest agony comes when Cordelia dies. By now Kent too welcomes death. His line 'Break heart; I prithee, break' might refer to Lear's suffering or his own (V.3.312).

## Progress booster: The causes of suffering       **A03**

It is important that you can identify what causes the intense suffering in *King Lear*. Gloucester thinks that the gods are sadistic; Lear wants to know why nature has given him two malignant daughters. However, you might feel that all the agony can be traced back, not to nature, but to human acts. Characters suffer for their own sins or because they are sinned against, even if they suffer disproportionately. At the end of the play the state too is in disarray, signified by the word 'gored' (V.3.320) and the storm can be seen as a metaphor for England's suffering as well as Lear's.

## Learning through suffering

Is anything learned through suffering? The good endure and help each other. Lear and Gloucester become more perceptive and compassionate. Edgar becomes stronger and fit to rule. Through suffering, these three male characters achieve heroism. In *King Lear* Shakespeare seems to suggest that it is man's fate to suffer and we must make the best of it.

### Key quotations: Lear's suffering                                      A01

Lear tells Cordelia, 'I am bound / Upon a wheel of fire' (IV.7.46–7). Still half asleep, he believes that he is in Hell, tied to an instrument of torture; we can take this as a **metaphor** for his suffering in this world.

## Natural and unnatural

### Study focus: Conflicting views of nature                              A02

On the heath Lear wants to know whether nature is responsible for his turmoil. The play does not provide straightforward answers. We are presented with conflicting views of what is natural. Edmund suggests that nature is a malevolent goddess who provides him with the bad attitudes necessary to challenge the status quo. Cruelty seems to come equally naturally to Goneril and Regan. For them, there is no given order; they seek to create their own selfish universe. However, the good characters see this trio as unnatural and appeal for help to a benign nature. Cordelia calls on the 'unpublished virtues of the earth' to restore Lear (IV.4.16). For Kent, the Fool, Edgar and Cordelia, it is natural to be loving, trusting and loyal.

### Lear and Gloucester's treatment of their children

Lear represents the natural order, but transgresses against it when he fails to recognise Cordelia's worthiness, falsely calling her 'a wretch whom Nature is ashamed / Almost t' acknowledge hers' (I.1.211–2). He compounds his mistake when he gives Goneril and Regan power. Gloucester errs in a similar fashion, disinheriting his legitimate heir in favour of the bastard, whom he mistakes for a 'Loyal and natural boy' (II.1.83). These errors are disastrous. Lear finds that his 'frame of nature' has been wrenched 'From the fixed place' (I.4.267–8). An enormous struggle ensues, as nature tries to reassert herself. The storm can be seen as both punishment and protest.

And yet, at the close of Act V, it is difficult to believe that nature is benevolent or that a natural order has really 'won'. Cordelia's death presents a problem for those who wish to see the end of *King Lear* as a triumph. Lear asks, 'Why should a dog, a horse, a rat have life, / And thou no breath at all?' (V.3.306–7). Perhaps we are meant to see Cordelia's death as the final punishment for Lear.

### Key quotations: The mystery of evil                                    A01

Lear struggles with the problem of evil: 'Is there any cause in nature that make these hard hearts?' (III.6.76–7). He cannot understand why Regan and Goneril have become so evil and, perhaps preferring not to consider his own responsibility, he wonders if there is some scientific explanation.

# Justice

## Human injustice

Throughout *King Lear* characters try to judge each other. Gloucester and Lear misjudge their children, whereas Cordelia has the measure of her sisters and Goneril and Regan's assessment of their father is acute. Edmund knows exactly how to take in his gullible relatives.

Gloucester's blinding is an appalling example of human injustice. Cornwall and Regan pervert the law to satisfy their own craving for revenge. Some see Cordelia's death as the greatest injustice in the play. Human judgement and the justice system look extremely fallible when the curtain goes down on Act V.

## Study focus: Flawed trials

**A02**

The 'trials' that occur in the play are all flawed. Lear's love-test is ill-conceived and has disastrous consequences. In Act II, the trial of Kent for plain-speaking is an excuse for Cornwall and Regan to exercise power arrogantly. Lear's mock trial of Goneril and Regan is attended by Poor Tom and a court jester, while the defendant is a joint-stool. This trial reminds us of the absurdity of Lear's actions in Act I Scene 1.

## Poetic and social justice

Fallibility is evident in the examples of unofficial or **poetic justice** that we see in the play. In Act V Scene 3 Edgar takes the law into his own hands when he challenges Edmund. We see poetic justice at work elsewhere: Cornwall is turned upon and killed by his own servant; Goneril and Regan are destroyed by their jealous lust; and Oswald too meets a sticky end. The thorniest question about justice concerns Gloucester and Lear. Do they deserve their punishments? Gloucester pays very dearly for his sins (although some of Shakespeare's contemporaries believed that blinding was the appropriate sentence for adultery). Lear suffers most when Cordelia is taken from him. Although his judgement and their loving relationship have both been restored by then, this comes too late for Lear.

*King Lear* is also concerned with social justice. Gloucester calls on the heavens to distribute wealth more evenly, while Lear considers the lives of the 'Poor naked wretches' he paid so little attention to (III.4.28–36). In Act IV, Lear rages against corrupt members of the judiciary and seems to sneer at himself and all those who presume to rule and judge others when he says, 'a dog's obeyed in office' (IV.6.157).

## A just conclusion?

At the end of the play we are presented with two new agents of justice, Albany and Edgar. We accept the justice of their actions in Act V Scene 3. But human judgement still looks faulty. Albany has almost been overwhelmed by events and Edgar's bitter words about Gloucester's death seem callous. Surely no one in *King Lear* is morally impeccable? Perhaps Shakespeare wants us to remain uncomfortable about justice.

**A04** **KEY CONNECTION**

There are many examples of revengers seeking justice in Renaissance drama. Many are dubious figures, like Vindice in Thomas Middleton's *The Revenger's Tragedy* or even Shakespeare's own Hamlet, but Edgar is a benign revenger, a figure of integrity who is driven to set things right.

## Key quotation: Harsh justice **A01**

Edgar accepts Gloucester's punishment, telling Edmund, 'The dark and vicious place where thee he got / Cost him his eyes' (V.3.172–3). Edgar is suggesting that his father deserved to be blinded for committing the act of adultery which brought Edmund into the world.

# Religion

## Lear and the gods

The characters make many appeals to the pagan deities in *King Lear*. Their attitudes towards the gods reflect their own natures and can also be linked to the theme of justice.

At the start of the play Lear believes that the gods are on his side. He expects them to punish Goneril and Regan. Later, however, Lear worries that the heavens are hostile and stir 'these daughters' hearts / Against their father' (II.4.273–4). By Act V he seems to have rediscovered his faith. We see the strength of Lear's love when he says it will take 'a brand from heaven' to part him and Cordelia (V.3.22). In fact, it is a mere mortal, Edmund, who deprives Lear of his beloved daughter. Lear makes no mention of the gods when he asks why Cordelia has been killed. His silence might be read as proof that man should be blamed for the carnage.

## The attitudes of Cordelia and Edgar

John J. Norton, in his essay 'King Lear and Protestantism' (in Hiscock and Hopkins, *King Lear: A Critical Guide*, 2011), argues that the action of the play reflects religious ideas that were current in Shakespeare's time. The theologians Luther, Calvin and Hooker all agreed that people must accept their own sinfulness and inability to redeem themselves before they could be saved by God. Lear's painful journey to humility can be taken as an example of this process, even though he lives in a pagan world which has not yet heard of salvation through Christ.

Other characters' attitudes to the gods make the issue of faith thornier still. What are we to make of Cordelia and Edgar, who behave with Christian fortitude and the virtues of patience, pity and benevolence? The religious **imagery** used to describe Cordelia in Act IV Scene 6 clearly identifies her as an example of Christian goodness. Cordelia sees the gods as kindly, calling on them to restore Lear's senses. But how can we believe the gods are just when her body is carried onto the stage directly after Albany's line 'The Gods defend her' (V.3.255)? At this moment we are likely to agree with Gloucester's pessimistic assessment of the gods; they seem capricious and sadistic. Edgar's faith presents problems, too. His statement, 'The Gods are just, and of our pleasant vices / Make instruments to plague us' does not ring true when Cordelia is hanged (V.3.170–1). And does his father really deserve to die for adultery?

# Study focus: Atheism in *King Lear*    A02

Is Shakespeare making a case for atheism in *King Lear*? We need to consider Edmund, who professes to worship nature but shows no respect for any religion. In Act II Scene 1 he mocks his father when he pretends to believe in 'the revenging Gods' (II.1.44). Even when he pants for life and decides to do good in Act V Scene 3, Edmund never suggests that his change of heart comes about because he suddenly believes in divine retribution. The speed of Edmund's rise and the fact that he is responsible for Cordelia's death suggest man is as powerful and cruel as any force above. However, Edmund's progress is eventually stopped by two god-fearing characters. The atheist is not allowed to defeat the faithful. Shakespeare refuses to provide us with any straightforward answers to the many questions we have about religion in *King Lear*.

# Key quotations: Despair    A01

After his blinding, Gloucester comments bitterly, 'As flies to wanton boys, are we to th'Gods; / They kill us for their sport' (IV.1.36–7). He can no longer believe that the gods are benevolent. Instead, he imagines them playing with human beings as some children torment insects, making them suffer for their entertainment.

# The family and feudalism

## A way of life breaks down

The Jacobean age was a time of social and religious change. The feudal, medieval view of the world was under scrutiny and traditional assumptions about gender and class were being questioned by many. With its focus on the king and his family, many contemporary critics believe that *King Lear* reflects the anxieties of the period. The play charts the breakdown – not just of a character – but of a whole way of life. Albany and Kent's opening lines hint that we are in a world of political uncertainty.

## Absolute authority

In Act I Scene 1 Lear behaves like a medieval monarch. He is used to wielding his power with absolute authority and expects meek obedience. When Kent challenges him he is outraged: 'On thine allegiance' he rages (I.1.166). He dismisses Cordelia with words which reflect his power, 'Better thou had not been born than not t' have pleased me better' (I.1.232–3), and 'be gone / Without our grace, our love, our benison' (I.2.263–4). When she is disinherited, Cordelia becomes a nonentity. She can only regain a position in the world when she is chosen in marriage by another man, who takes her without that **symbol** of her father's power, her dowry. Lear's medieval absolutism is already being undermined.

## Study focus: A new age? **A02**

Consider the effect of Lear's actions on the hierarchy of the state. When he rejects Cordelia, Lear plunges his family and community into crisis. He allows a new breed of opportunists to undermine the hierarchy. It is a measure of the strength of the new breed that they get as far as they do. Goneril, Regan and Edmund will not accept the roles allotted to them – Goneril and Regan refuse to behave like good, submissive Renaissance women should, and Edmund will not be marginalised. All three grasp at and enjoy exercising power. They show no respect for the family or the state. Even when they are vanquished in Act V, the restored hierarchy looks shaky. The first family lies dead on the stage. The survivors are all numb, hardly ready to sustain the 'gored' state (V.3.320).

## Key quotation: The sense of crisis **A01**

Gloucester laments, 'We have seen the best of our time: machinations, hollowness, treachery, and all ruinous disorders follow us disquietly to out graves' (I.2.114–7).

## Revision task 7: Ecocriticism **A05**

Anthony Parr has suggested that, given its attention to conflicting ideas of 'nature', *King Lear* might be considered from an ecological perspective.

Make a list of moments in the play which could be interpreted from this point of view. For example, when Lear divides up the country for the love-test, he sees 'our kingdom' (I.1.37) purely as property which he can dispose of as he pleases, with no apparent regard for guardianship of the land or for the welfare of the creatures who reside there.

**A03** KEY CONTEXT

Renaissance society was patriarchal and gerontocratic (controlled by elderly men); men did not consider retirement, nor did they pass on their power and wealth when they reached old age. They retained their power until they died. Lear and Gloucester continue to wield power even when their judgement is failing and, in the eyes of some of their children, are obstacles preventing a younger generation from succeeding to power.

**A03** KEY CONTEXT

The rituals that we see Lear trying to act out in Act I Scene 1 mirror the ceremonial public rituals that English culture demanded. Elizabeth I and James I expected their subjects to kneel, bow and scrape as marks of respect.

........................................................................................

# PROGRESS CHECK

........................................................................................

## Section One: Check your understanding

These tasks will help you to evaluate your knowledge and skills level in this particular area.

1. List the ways in which Lear's love-test might be considered irrational and irresponsible.
2. How thoroughly does Edmund reject the social hierarchy? Write a paragraph assessing his attitude.
3. How does the animal imagery which is applied to Goneril and Regan shape our view of them? Examine three examples, allocating one paragraph to each.
4. List reasons which might account for the Fool's disappearance after Act III Scene 6.
5. Write a paragraph on how Albany changes during the course of the play.
6. Summarise in a couple of paragraphs the importance of clothing and nudity in the play.
7. Find three examples of different ways in which the word 'nothing' is used and comment on them.
8. Why do you think so many people have been shocked by the death of Cordelia? Give three reasons.
9. The Folio version of the play omits Lear's mock trial of Goneril and Regan. Write a paragraph discussing what might be lost by its removal.
10. Give three examples of how the characters' references to the gods are undermined.

**PROGRESS BOOSTER**   **A01**

For each Section Two task, read the question carefully, select the key areas you need to address, and plan an essay of six to seven points. Write a first draft, giving yourself an hour to do so. Make sure you include supporting evidence for each point, including quotations.

## Section Two: Working towards the exam

Choose one of the following three tasks which require longer, more developed answers:

1. How sympathetic a character do you find Lear? How might an audience's response to him change during the course of the play?
2. Explore the differences and similarities we see in the characters of Edmund and Edgar.
3. It has been said that *King Lear* is a play in which madness leads to greater understanding of the truth. To what extent do you agree with this observation?

| Progress check | | | | | |
|---|---|---|---|---|---|
| (rate your understanding on a level of 1 – low, to 5 – high) | **1** | **2** | **3** | **4** | **5** |
| How the main characters contribute to the action, themes and ideas | | | | | |
| How the minor characters contribute to the action, themes and ideas | | | | | |
| The different ways each character can be interpreted in terms of Shakespeare's presentation of them | | | | | |
| What the key themes of the play are | | | | | |
| How the key themes reflect wider ideas about society and human nature | | | | | |

## GENRE

### Tragedy

**Tragedy** originated in Greece in the fifth century BC as a form of drama which, by tracing the downfall of an individual (the protagonist), shows both the potential greatness and painful vulnerability of human existence. The individual concerned is generally an important, larger-than-life person such as a leader, whose fall affects those around them. The fall may be due in part to a character flaw or error of judgement, though the tragic hero may also seem to be sacrificed for the common good, giving them aspects of both villain and victim.

Ancient Greek tragedy was staged partly as a religious rite, partly as a dramatic competition. The actors wore masks which amplified their voices and high shoes to make them prominent, and were accompanied by a **chorus**, a group of characters representing ordinary people who chanted and danced comments on the action.

### Aristotle's *Poetics*

In the fourth century BC the philosopher Aristotle discussed tragedy influentially in his *Poetics*. Aristotle's teacher Plato had criticised storytelling and even music for arousing harmful emotions, but Aristotle argued that tragedy aroused pity and fear only in order to get them out of our systems. The climax of the play gave us a purification or 'catharsis' of these emotions. Aristotle also noted that the protagonist's downfall is linked to his fatal error or 'hamartia' and pointed out that his story will typically include reversals of fortune ('peripeteia') and moments of discovery ('anagnorisis').

### The Shakespearean era

The tragedy of Shakespeare's era was influenced by the Roman poet Seneca, whose bloodthirsty descriptions are echoed in Thomas Kyd's *Spanish Tragedy* and Shakespeare's own *Titus Andronicus*. Although Christopher Marlowe and John Webster wrote notable tragedies, Shakespeare's *Hamlet*, *King Lear*, *Othello* and *Macbeth* are the most outstanding of the era, along with his more romantic *Romeo and Juliet* and *Antony and Cleopatra*.

**(A02)**

## Study focus: *King Lear* as tragedy

In many respects, *King Lear* corresponds to the tragedy genre by showing a flawed character initiating his own downfall and struggling heroically to cope with the suffering he has unleashed. The Fool comments like a chorus. Lear's destruction has terrible repercussions for his family and the whole nation. His somewhat irresponsible attitude to governing the country seems to be expunged when Edgar replaces him. However, Shakespeare elaborates his story beyond the tragic formula, using, for example, the Gloucester **subplot** to reinforce the themes, comedy to vary the tone and the story of Edgar's ascent to counterpoint Lear's decline.

**(A01) PROGRESS BOOSTER**

In writing about *King Lear*, avoid using the features of the tragedy genre simply as a checklist to record which ones the play displays and which ones seem to be absent. Compiling a list will not be considered a thoughtful, critical response and will not attract marks. Instead, your aim should be to discuss how Shakespeare has developed the features of tragedy to create powerful drama, focusing on the details of the play itself.

## Revision task 8: Tragedy     **(A05)**

Write a paragraph explaining what makes Lear a tragic figure. Are there any other characters who might be regarded as tragic? If so, do the same for them, noting how their situation is similar to – or different from – Lear's situation.

# STRUCTURE

## The five Acts

Because all editions of *King Lear* present the play in five Acts, many critics have used this division to navigate through the story, labelling the five parts in turn as an initial action, rising complications, a climax or turning point, a movement towards resolution and a final outcome (or 'catastrophe'). While this five-Act approach has benefits, it is not clear that Shakespeare himself had it in mind. Act divisions became common only towards the end of his career and the Act headings of *Lear* were not included till the Folio edition, in a decision apparently made by the editors after Shakespeare's death. The critic Fredson Bowers has suggested that, far from following this conventional structure, Shakespeare actually begins with the climax (the love-test) and devotes the rest of the play to following its **tragic** consequences, through to the catastrophe of Cordelia's death.

## Study focus: The subplot

It is important you can write about how the use of an elaborate **subplot** distinguishes *King Lear* from Shakespeare's other tragedies. The story of Gloucester and his sons adds variety of action, allows themes to be explored in more depth, produces greater suspense as the two plots interact, and supplies the story of Lear and his daughters with a villain (Edmund) and a hero (Edgar). If asked, most people would probably recall that the play begins with Lear's love-test, but in fact Shakespeare introduces Gloucester and Edmund before it takes place, suggesting how important it is to him that the two plots should run side by side throughout.

The primacy of the **main plot** is established by allocating far more space to it in the first half of the play. At the end, the entry of Lear with Cordelia in his arms restores the Lear plot to prominence just when Edmund and Edgar are threatening to monopolise our interest. Edmund is carried away to die undramatically off-stage and Edgar's elevation to the throne in the final lines is overshadowed by Lear's powerful death scene.

## The scenes

The individual scene, focused on the present, is Shakespeare's basic unit of structure. He does not give us the realistic, detailed background which we might find in a modern novel. We do not know, for example, how Lear and Gloucester raised such divergent children, nor how their wives came to die. Instead, Shakespeare offers a series of dramatic scenes which place the characters into challenging situations and shows us vividly how they react, in so doing revealing their personalities and moving the story forwards.

### Revision task 9: Plot and subplot

Draw up a chart so that you can see clearly how the main plot and subplot interact. One way to do this would be to draw three columns and go through the play scene by scene, putting the story of Lear and his daughters in one, that of Gloucester and his sons in another and their overlap in the third. Do you see a pattern emerge?

## LANGUAGE

### Study focus: Blank verse and rhyme

*King Lear* is written in **blank verse** and prose. Blank verse consists of unrhymed iambic pentameters – lines with five stresses, with the stresses mostly falling on the even syllables ('Come *on*, my *boy*. How *dost,* my *boy?* Art *cold*?' III.2.680). You will notice that Shakespeare does not stick to the rules of blank verse rigidly. He varies the rhythm to avoid monotony, to make the speeches sound more life-like and to emphasise key words ('*Hear, Nature, hear*! dear *God*dess, *hear*!', I.4.274).

In order to make the rhythm flow more naturally, syllables are often elided (run together), e.g. *over* often becomes *o'er* and *it is* becomes *'tis*. Shakespeare also uses shorter lines for emphasis (you will find many examples of this, especially during tense moments or scenes of chaos). Longer lines are used to avoid the comic sing-song or monotonous effect of repeated iambic pentameters.

At the end of scenes, Shakespeare sometimes uses rhyming couplets to provide a sense of closure and to make it clear to the audience, in the absence of scenery or a curtain, that the action is about to move to a new location. Rhyme is also used to draw attention to particular thoughts or ideas. The Fool's songs and proverbs are examples of this.

### Verse and prose

'Low' or comic characters generally speak in prose in Elizabethan and Jacobean drama. Traditionally, scenes of 'madness' were also written in prose. Shakespeare obeys these conventions in *King Lear*, but you will notice that prose is used on other occasions too. Sometimes scenes contain both verse and prose. We would expect Lear to speak in verse because he is a king. However, as his wits desert him, he shifts from verse to prose and back again, signifying the disruption in his mind. You will also notice that Lear uses the third person (the royal 'we') early in the play, but adopts the more humble first person ('I', 'methinks') when he recognises that he is powerless. This change reflects his change in status, from king to 'a foolish old man'.

You might want to consider the dramatic effects of other language choices. For example, why does Gloucester enter in Act I Scene 2 muttering in prose? Perhaps Shakespeare wants to show how troubled Gloucester is as he feverishly considers recent events. The swift-moving prose also perhaps anticipates Gloucester's hasty decision-making later in the scene.

### Simple language

The language of *King Lear* – especially the final scene – is direct and simple, with the exception of Edgar's rantings and the Fool's riddles. Lear's words over Cordelia's body, 'She's dead as earth' (V.3.261), bring home the dreadful truth of her loss and move us more than any complicated speech could do. This simplicity in the face of horror is an integral part of the play's dramatic power, as are two other conventions: characters use **asides** and **soliloquies** to inform the audience about their feelings and intentions, drawing us into their world.

**A03 KEY CONTEXT**

Seemingly familiar words may have shifted in meaning over the last four centuries. When Cordelia says she is 'unhappy' (I.1.90), she actually means that she is 'unfortunate', and the word 'practice' (II.1.72 and V.3.151) refers to a nasty scheme or a trick, a meaning it still retains in the expressions 'sharp practice' and 'practical joke'.

When Edgar confides to the audience, 'My tears begin to take his part' (III.6.60), as well as his shift to normal speech reminding us that he is not really Poor Tom, the aside emphasises how shocking it is for someone to witness a king lose his mind and shows us that Edgar is a person with a generous spirit, able to care about someone else's suffering even in the midst of his own danger and degradation.

## Progress booster: Personal styles

Make sure that you can write about how Shakespeare's characters have their own personal 'styles', reflecting their roles, emotions and natures. For example, Goneril and Regan use clipped commands, which demonstrate their craving for power. Kent points out that he has to use 'other accents' to disguise his speech once he has been banished (I.4.1). Most actors who play Kent do this by adopting a rough, country accent. No longer a great earl, Kent has to hide his identity, but does little to modify the blunt, downright expressions of opinion that are characteristic of him.

Kent is not alone in adopting a false voice in order to escape detection. As Poor Tom, Edgar takes as his model the 'roaring voices' (II.3.14) of the mentally disturbed, speaking obsessive thoughts aloud in an alarming fashion. Later, as he moves away from the danger zone of his father's house, he feels confident enough to become 'better spoken' (IV.6.10), then, confronted by a sword-wielding Oswald, switches to a West Country accent, causing his opponent to mistake him for an ignorant yokel unschooled in the art of sword-fighting. He closes the play with a thoughtful speech which shows him to be in command of himself, the situation and indeed the country. When he uses the pronoun 'we' four times in just three lines, is he speaking on behalf of all those on stage or adopting the royal 'we' appropriate for a king?

## Obscure language

There are two kinds of language in the play which are particularly difficult for us to follow. One is the comic banter of the Fool, the other is the ranting of Edgar when he is being Poor Tom. While much of the Fool's quick-fire wit remains accessible and sharply comic, his references to songs, proverbs and slang expressions have lost much of their significance. Shakespeare's original audience were probably amused when they heard the Fool parody a solemn, religious song, 'Some men for sudden joy do weep' (I.4.171), but a modern actor taking the role of the Fool knows he will not get that reaction today and needs to supply comic behaviour to compensate. Fortunately, we can follow the Fool's line of thought sufficiently clearly to appreciate his point of view and his humour; the 'mad' speeches present a greater challenge.

Once Lear breaks down, his rapid switches of topic can be hard to follow. He often thinks dramatically, conjuring up characters and scenes. However, with careful reading and help from an editor's notes, we can still follow most of what he says. Edgar, however, acts the part of a 'madman' so thoroughly that he often leaves us baffled. It is doubtful whether even Shakespeare's original audience would have understood 'suum, mun, hey no nonny. Dolphin my boy, boy; cessa! let him trot by' (III.4.101–2). What these words do convey to us is the extremity of Edgar's feelings. He cannot risk speaking openly, so he rants nonsense with all the passion of his anger and anxiety. When he responds to his father's presence by muttering, 'Poor Tom's a-cold' (III.4.148), his own misery comes through to us clearly.

# Animal and other imagery

## Study focus: Savage creatures

There is a wealth of animal **imagery** in *King Lear*. The most important recurring references are to savage creatures, which are associated with Goneril and Regan. The sisters are also likened to fiends and monsters. Goneril is 'sharp-toothed … like a vulture' (II.4.133), with a 'wolfish visage' (I.4.305). Lear curses her as a 'detested kite!' (I.4.261) and tells Regan she looked 'most serpent-like' upon him (II.4.158–9). Gloucester says the sisters possess 'boarish fangs' (III.7.57) and Albany eventually sees them as 'Tigers, not daughters' (IV.2.40), who behave like 'monsters of the deep' (IV.2.49). Even Edmund, who is himself described as a 'toad-spotted traitor', speaks of them using animal imagery (V.3.138). They are jealous as 'the stung / Are of the adder' (V.1.56–7). Their sexuality is as abhorrent as their cruelty. Lear describes women as living 'centaurs' (IV.6.123).

The implications of all these references are clear: Goneril and Regan are cruel predators, 'pelican daughters' who want to see their father bleed (III.4.76). Their inhumanity is reconfirmed when Gloucester and Cordelia describe how a wild beast would have been allowed shelter in the storm, but not Lear (III.7.61–2 and IV.7.36–40). Appropriately, Goneril and Regan are destroyed by their animal instincts.

## Other animals

There are other references to animals which help us understand Lear's plight. The Fool uses telling imagery when he says to Lear 'the hedge-sparrow fed the cuckoo so long / That it's had it head bit off by it young' (I.4.214–5). The image of Lear as a hedge-sparrow emphasises his vulnerability. Like Poor Tom, Edgar dwells on the way he is stalked by devils, recalling the way Lear is treated by Goneril and Regan. Reduced to an abject state on the heath, Lear claims that man is a 'poor, bare, forked animal' (III.4.110).

Lear's vulnerability is emphasised at the start of the final scene when the king pictures life in prison, where he and Cordelia will 'sing like birds in a cage' (V.3.9). For the first time, in the final scene of the play, we are presented with an attractive animal image. However, song-birds are passive, tame creatures. This image hints how much Lear's visions of happiness are deluded.

**A01** PROGRESS BOOSTER

Animal imagery recurs throughout *King Lear*, but there are other images which can be fruitfully discussed. Consider, for example, images to do with the body. In a story where people are stripped of titles, defences, houses and even clothes, and where humanity seems a 'poor, bare, forked animal' (III.4.110), images of eyes and hands, the body and the diseases that infect it, all help to create an atmosphere of vulnerability.

# PROGRESS CHECK

## Section One: Check your understanding

These tasks will help you to evaluate your knowledge and skills level in this particular area.

1. A tragedy commonly includes reversals of fortune and moments of discovery. Find three examples of each in the play and comment on the audience's likely reactions to them.

2. Write a couple of paragraphs comparing Lear and Gloucester as tragic figures.

3. Lear's flaw (or hamartia) has been described as arrogance, overvaluation of appearance, lack of self-knowledge and lack of self-control. Write a paragraph explaining your own view of his weakness.

4. If you had to divide the play into three sections, separated by two intervals, where would you place the breaks and why? Give three reasons.

5. Note three occasions where the noble characters switch to prose and for each example suggest why Shakespeare might have made that decision.

6. Find five asides in the play and suggest why each was included.

7. Look at how the word 'nothing' is used in the play and write a paragraph summing up its significance. (An online text with a search facility will help with this.)

8. Copy or print out a key speech, such as Lear's 'Blow, winds' (III.2.1–9), and annotate it, advising the actor on how the lines should best be spoken.

9. Look at how the words 'nature' and 'natural' are used in the play. List as many different meanings of them as you can find and note who uses them in which contexts.

10. On stage, words and action go together. Open the play at random and make notes on what movements, gestures and expressions the actor might make in delivering the lines that you find there.

## Section Two: Working towards the exam

Choose one of the following three tasks which require longer, more developed answers:

1. 'Without the subplot of Gloucester and his sons, *King Lear* would be a much poorer play.' To what extent do you agree?

2. How do the comic elements in the play support the tragedy, rather than detract from it?

3. '*King Lear* is a tragedy of political power, but also a family tragedy.' Discuss.

**PROGRESS BOOSTER**    **A01**

For each Section Two task, read the question carefully, select the key areas you need to address, and plan an essay of six to seven points. Write a first draft, giving yourself an hour to do so. Make sure you include supporting evidence for each point, including quotations.

| Progress check | | | | | |
|---|---|---|---|---|---|
| (rate your understanding on a level of 1 – low, to 5 – high) | 1 | 2 | 3 | 4 | 5 |
| How the play can be located within the genre of tragedy | | | | | |
| How the Gloucester subplot enhances the themes of the play | | | | | |
| How Shakespeare employs blank verse and prose | | | | | |
| The different kinds of language used in different parts of the play | | | | | |
| What key images tell us about the characters | | | | | |

## CONTEXTS

### Historical context

#### Nothing beyond question

Shakespeare arrived in London at the start of a 'golden age' for English literature, a development within that cultural movement which we call the 'Renaissance'. Meaning literally 'rebirth', the word refers to a revival of artistic and intellectual endeavour which began in Italy in the fourteenth century.

The rediscovery of many Classical texts and the culture of Greece and Rome fostered great confidence in human reason and potential, which was shown in many different fields. The discovery of America demonstrated that the world was a larger and stranger place than had been thought. Arguments that the sun, not the earth, was the centre of our planetary system challenged the centuries-old belief that humans were at the centre of the cosmos. The political philosophy of Machiavelli seemed to cut politics free from morality. And the religious movements we know collectively as the Reformation set the individual conscience, not church authority, at the centre of the religious life. Nothing, it seemed, was beyond questioning, nothing impossible.

Shakespeare's drama, too, questions the beliefs and assumptions upon which Elizabethan society was founded. The plays always conclude in a restoration of order, as audience expectation and censorship required, but many critics argue that Shakespeare's imaginative energy goes into subverting, rather than reinforcing, traditional values. For example, King Lear believes himself to embody natural authority, with a divine right comparable to that claimed by Shakespeare's King James I, yet events show him to be a fallible old man whose deteriorating mind brings about the destruction of his family and threatens the whole nation. He and Gloucester come to realise that their society is an unjust one, where the rich flourish at the expense of the poor and the powerful are free to punish the weak while keeping their own sins hidden. Prayers go unanswered; help comes only to those strong enough to help themselves. *King Lear* evades the charge of subversion by being set in the distant past, but it certainly has implications for the state of the nation in Shakespeare's time.

**A03**

## Study focus: The state of the nation

Many of Shakespeare's plays show how preoccupied he was with national identity. His history plays examine how the England of the time came into being through the conflicts of the fifteenth century. He was fascinated by the exercise of power, bringing critical perspectives to bear, in particular on the royal court. The court's hypocrisy may be bitterly denounced (for example, in Lear's diatribes) and its self-seeking ambition represented in the figure of a **Machiavellian** villain (such as Edmund). Courtiers are frequently figures of fun whose unmanly sophistication is contrasted with plain-speaking integrity: Oswald set against Kent, for example. Direct criticism of the monarch or the contemporary English court would not be tolerated; this may be one reason why Shakespeare's plays were always set in the past or abroad.

Niccolò Machiavelli

**A03** **KEY CONTEXT**

*King Lear* was written during a time of uncertainty and unrest. In 1606, the year that the play was first performed, London had been badly hit by the plague, which shut the theatres. In 1605, Guy Fawkes' plot to blow up Parliament and kill James I had been foiled.

**A03** **KEY CONTEXT**

In Shakespeare's London there were between five and eight theatres open at any one time. Audience figures were very large, with 18,000 to 24,000 people visiting the theatre each week.

### Religion

The nationalism of the English Renaissance was reinforced by Henry VIII's break with Rome. The ensuing disputes between Protestants and Catholics fostered religious scepticism. Shakespeare's plays are remarkably free from direct religious sentiment, leading many to question where his sympathies, if any, lie. His tragic heroes are haunted by their consciences, seeking their true selves, agonising over what course of action to take as they embark on a kind of spiritual journey. As *King Lear* is set in a pre-Christian Britain, it can sidestep religious controversies. Edmund's blasphemy and Gloucester's suicidal despair would be unacceptable if placed in the mouths of Christians.

# Shakespeare's theatre

### The dramatists

The theatre for which the plays were written was one of the most remarkable innovations of the Renaissance. During the medieval period plays had been almost exclusively religious, performed on carts and in open spaces at Christian festivals. Professional performers offered only mimes, juggling and comedy acts. They were regarded by officialdom and polite society as little better than vagabonds and layabouts. Those employed by the nobility, like Lear's fool, were the fortunate exceptions.

Just before Shakespeare went to London, all this began to change. A number of young men who had been to the universities of Oxford and Cambridge came to London in the 1580s and began to write plays that made use of what they had learned about the Classical drama of ancient Greece and Rome. Plays such as Christopher Marlowe's *Tamburlaine the Great* (about 1587) and Thomas Kyd's *The Spanish Tragedy* (1588–9) were unlike anything that had been written in English before. They were full-length plays on secular subjects, taking their plots from history and legend, adopting many of the devices of the Classical theatre, and offering a range of characterisation and situation hitherto unknown in English drama. With the exception of the prose dramas of John Lyly, these plays were composed in **blank verse** (unrhymed iambic pentameters), a freer and more expressive medium than the rhymed verse of medieval drama.

### Professional theatre

The most significant change of all, however, was that these dramatists wrote for the professional theatre. In 1576 James Burbage built the first permanent theatre in England, in Shoreditch, just beyond London's northern boundary. It was called simply 'The Theatre'. Others soon followed. So when Shakespeare came to London, there was a flourishing drama scene, with theatres and companies of actors. His company performed at James Burbage's Theatre until 1596, and used the Swan and Curtain until they moved into their own new theatre, the Globe, in 1599. It was burned down in 1613 when a cannon was fired during a performance of Shakespeare's *Henry VIII*, and was rebuilt in 1614.

### The Globe

With the completion in 1996 of Sam Wanamaker's project to construct in London a replica of the Globe, a version of Shakespeare's theatre can now be experienced at first hand. It is very different from the usual modern experience of drama. The form of the Elizabethan theatre derived from the inn yards and animal baiting rings in which actors had performed previously. They were circular wooden buildings with a paved courtyard in the middle, open to the sky. A rectangular stage jutted out into the middle of this yard. Some of the audience

---

**KEY CONTEXT**  (A03)

Plays were not generally considered to be serious literature in this period. When in 1612 Sir Thomas Bodley was setting up his library in Oxford, he instructed his staff not to buy any drama for the collection: 'haply [perhaps] some plays may be worthy, but hardly one in forty.'

---

**KEY CONTEXT**  (A03)

For a detailed and dramatic account of the creation of the Globe, which included dismantling The Theatre against the opposition of the landowner, see James Shapiro's *1599: A Year in the Life of William Shakespeare* (2005).

stood in the yard (or 'pit') to watch the play. They were thus on three sides of the stage, close up to it and on a level with it. These 'groundlings' paid only a penny to get in, but for wealthier spectators there were seats in three covered tiers or galleries between the inner and outer walls of the building, extending round most of the auditorium and overlooking the pit and the stage.

## Staging practices

A theatre like the Globe could hold about three thousand spectators. The yards were about 80ft in diameter and the rectangular stage approximately 40ft by 30ft and 5ft 6in high. Shakespeare called such a theatre a 'wooden O' in the prologue to *Henry V* (line 13). The stage itself was partially covered by a roof or canopy, which projected from the wall at the rear of the stage and was supported by two posts at the front. This protected the stage and performers from bad weather, and to it were secured winches and other machinery for stage effects. On either side at the back of the stage was a door. These led into the dressing room (or 'tiring house') and it was by means of these doors that actors entered and left the stage. Between the doors was a small recess or alcove which was curtained off.

There was very little in the way of scenery or props – there was nowhere to store them (there were no wings in this theatre) nor any way to set them up. Also, productions had to be transportable for performance at court or at noble houses. The stage was bare, which is why characters often tell us where they are. In *King Lear* II.3.2–3, for example, Edgar explains he has just climbed out of a tree where he has been hiding; we cannot be shown it. The bareness of the stage is also why location is so often **symbolic**. It suggests a dramatic mood or situation, rather than a place: Lear's barren heath reflects his destitute state, as the storm does his emotional turmoil.

## Continuous action

The staging of Elizabethan plays was continuous, with the many short 'scenes' of which Shakespeare's plays are often constructed following one after another in quick succession. We have to think of a more fluid, and much faster, production than we are generally used to: in the prologues to *Romeo and Juliet* (line 12) and *Henry VIII* (line 13) Shakespeare speaks of the playing time as only two hours. It is because plays were staged continuously that exits and entrances are written in as part of the script: characters speak as they enter or leave the stage because otherwise there would be a silence while, in full view, they took up their positions. This is also why dead bodies like that of the servant who stabs Cornwall have to be carried off (III.7.94–5).

**A03** **KEY CONTEXT**

We do not know much about the props used by theatre companies in Shakespeare's time, although the evidence we do have suggests there were some quite ambitious examples. One list dating from 1598 includes decorated cloths depicting cities or the night sky, items of armour, horses' heads and 'one hell mouth', probably for performances of Marlowe's famous play *Doctor Faustus*.

# Settings

## The court

The play opens with court gossip of the kind Lear will later learn to mock as chatter about 'who's in, who's out' (V.3.15). Is Albany or Cornwall now in the King's favour? What scandal must Gloucester answer to? In this self-regarding world, where the rest of the country is shrunk to a map for the king to dispose of, Lear is absolute ruler. We see everyone come onto the stage in hierarchical order and kneel before him, awaiting his decisions. Most flatter and obey him; even Cordelia and Kent have his interests at heart. Only Edmund, who has been 'out nine years' (I.1.31), has a different perspective. He senses the princesses' frustration, Cornwall's ambition, the older generation's complacency. Later, at Albany's castle, Lear finds that his power is frailer than he appreciated and experiences the humiliation of being downgraded from majesty to annoying guest.

## Gloucester's castle

In the first half of the play the characters converge on Gloucester's residence (which most editions assume to be a castle.) Here, the story enters a new phase, as the old hierarchy is overthrown. Edmund traps his half-brother in his lodging, then releases him to be hunted down. Regan and Cornwall visit only to avoid their obligations to Lear, then show their true colours when they take control, expel the old king and mutilate their host. The king and his few shabby followers are reduced to hiding in an outhouse before Gloucester arranges Lear's escape.

## The countryside

A favourite device of Shakespeare's comedies is a shift between the court and an alternative pastoral world of fertility and renewal. The countryside has a comparable function in *King Lear*, but presents a challenge rather than an escape. Beyond Gloucester's house stretches a barren land with 'scarce a bush' (II.4.301), where Lear is exposed to the terrible storm. The landscape **symbolises** the inhospitable reality with which Lear must come to terms. The only shelter is the hovel where Edgar hides, reminding Lear that for the homeless people he has neglected such squalor is a normal part of existence. Lear loses all sense of reality, but Edgar merely pretends to break down. He vents his emotions in crazy talk but adapts to raw nature with determination, hiding in a tree from his pursuers and defying the 'winds and persecutions of the sky' (II.3.12).

## Dover

In the second half of the play the characters converge on Dover, where Cordelia has landed in a doomed attempt to restore the old order that her father once controlled. Our strongest image of the area comes when Edgar invents a view from the clifftop to trick his father, imposing his human priorities on the natural world. Far away from the civilisation of the court, Lear, Cordelia, Edmund, Goneril, Regan and Oswald all die beside the battlefield. Edgar and Albany are left facing the challenge of how to reconstruct a just and peaceful Britain.

# Literary context

## Contemporary connections

Elizabethan and Jacobean plays originated with a comparatively small group of authors, who worked in the same theatrical culture and often knew one another professionally. Not surprisingly, they employed common themes; this creates scope to compare *King Lear* to other plays.

## Good and evil

The play *Doctor Faustus* by Christopher Marlowe (c. 1592), about a scholar who sells his soul to the devil, draws on the old medieval morality plays. Just as the central character of a morality play was addressed by symbolic figures of virtue and vice who directed his soul towards heaven or hell, so Faustus is counselled by Good and Evil Angels. Gloucester is similarly advised by Edgar and Edmund, one trying to save his soul, one sending him towards destruction. Meanwhile, Lear's love-test and division of the kingdom set him on the path to tragedy just as Faustus's contract with the devil does, and leave him with a similar, grim task of coming to terms with what he has done. And like Faustus, Edmund casts aside traditional restraints and morality in the name of personal ambition, with at times a disturbingly heroic quality.

## Madness

Madness was a popular subject with playwrights of the time, offering dramatic behaviour on stage as well as a way of depicting a world gone wrong. In *The Duchess of Malfi* by John Webster (1614), a tragedy in which the widowed Duchess is tormented and murdered by her two brothers, one of them, Ferdinand, confronts her with 'several sorts of madmen', each nursing an obsession, as indeed Ferdinand himself seems to do for her. Shakespeare's account of Poor Tom and the breakdown of Lear are far more sympathetic and thoughtful than Webster's treatment of madness. However, Webster's treatment of Antonio, the Duchess's steward whom she secretly marries, is far more sympathetic than Shakespeare's of Oswald or of the upstart Edmund. Both tragedies are, nonetheless, propelled by family breakdown.

## Modern connections

Given the influence of Shakespeare, and the timelessness of themes such as personal, family and political breakdown, it is not surprising that comparisons can also be made between *King Lear* and more recent plays. In *A Streetcar Named Desire* by Tennessee Williams (1947), the central character, Blanche, is an outcast whose disturbed speeches offer insights into the conventions and power structures of society. A victim of brutal domestic violence, she is betrayed by her family and suffers a mental breakdown. There are parallels here with Lear, Gloucester and Edgar, while Stanley, her brother-in-law, resembles Edmund in being a ruthless social upstart, determined to prevail at any cost.

Brian Friel's play *The Home Place* (2005), set in an English household in Ireland in the late nineteenth century, shows institutionalised neglect of the poor and generational conflict (the father and son both in love with the same woman). An unequal match (between the son David and the housekeeper Margaret) is the only sign of hope in a world moving towards the civil war and terrorism which will break out in the following century.

**A03** **KEY CONNECTION**

A notable performance of *Doctor Faustus* staged at the Globe in 2011, featuring Paul Hilton and Arthur Darvill, has been made available as a DVD. A number of excellent adaptations of *A Streetcar Named Desire* are also available. The most famous one, which it should be noted contains alterations to the text to shorten the running time and play down the most disturbing elements, is the 1951 film version starring Marlon Brando and Vivien Leigh.

# CRITICAL INTERPRETATIONS

## Critical history

### Seventeenth-century criticsm

During Shakespeare's lifetime *King Lear* does not appear to have been as popular as *Hamlet* or *Macbeth*. In 1681 it was rewritten by Nahum Tate, who felt that the ending was too gloomy and the structure disorganised. His version of *King Lear* includes a happy ending (Lear does not die) and a romance between Edgar and Cordelia.

### Eighteenth-century criticsm

In 1753 Joseph Wharton objected to the Gloucester **subplot** as unlikely and distracting, and judged Gloucester's blinding too horrible to be staged. Wharton also found Goneril and Regan's savagery unbelievable. While Samuel Johnson (1768) accepted as realistic the way in which 'the wicked prosper and the virtuous miscarry', he took Shakespeare to task for lack of justice at the conclusion, finding Cordelia's death deeply shocking

### Nineteenth-century criticsm

Charles Lamb (1811) thought *King Lear* unactable. August Wilhelm Schlegel (1808) saw a drama in which 'humanity is stripped of all external and internal advantages, and given up prey to naked helplessness'. William Hazlitt (1817) noted the way in which the unnatural comes to dominate, but also believed that Shakespeare showed a 'firm faith in filial piety'. At the end of the century, the poet Swinburne (1880) was struck by the fatalism of Shakespeare's vision. Other Victorian critics saw grandeur and strength in the play, and Lear continued to trouble and move them. *King Lear* was now recognised as a great literary achievement. For George Brandes (1895), Cordelia was 'the living emblem of womanly dignity', while the play as a whole portrayed 'the titanic tragedy of human life'.

### Early twentieth-century criticsm

A. C. Bradley's *Shakespearean Tragedy* (1905) focused on character and motivation through close reading, treating Shakespearean tragedy as the suffering of an individual coming to terms with his personality. Implicitly taking the modern novel as his narrative model, Bradley commented on the play's careless inconsistencies, the loose episodic structure and the unwieldy subplot. However, he also conceded that the play was 'one of the world's greatest poems'. For him Lear was a superior figure whose heart-rending suffering was essentially unfathomable. Although Bradley's emphasis on character has been rejected by recent critics, many would agree that *King Lear* remains impossible to pin down.

In 1930, G. Wilson Knight's *The Wheel of Fire* explored the cruelty in the play, concluding that its effect was increased by an 'element of comedy'. Up to now, there had been very little emphasis on this aspect.

The question of whether or not *King Lear* can be interpreted as a 'Christian play' has troubled many critics. Some see Cordelia as a Christ-like figure and find Christian virtues in Edgar and Lear. Others disagree. For example, Kenneth Muir suggests in his *Penguin Critical Studies: King Lear* (1986) that Shakespeare excludes gods and an afterlife: 'It follows that human beings are entirely responsible for their actions, and that if these lead to disaster, the tragedy is absolute.' However, Muir also notes that many characters do seek to do good, regardless of the chaos that surrounds them.

# Contemporary approaches

More recently, scholars have become interested in the political and social implications of *King Lear*. Debate focuses on class, gender, race, the family, authority, the structures of power, and the meanings and functions of literary criticism itself. Some of the most interesting work on *King Lear* has come from **new historicist** and **feminist** critics.

## New historicist criticism

New historicists compare works of literature with non-literary writings of the same period in an attempt to understand their original contexts. In *Radical Tragedy* (1984), Jonathan Dollimore completely reassesses *King Lear*. For him, the play is not about the heroism of human endurance, or the moral growth of a hero who comes to know himself more thoroughly. Dollimore moves away from the analysis of character and individual suffering favoured by Bradley. He suggests that Lear's identity is a social construction: 'What makes Lear the person he is – or rather was – is not kingly essence (divine right), but, among other things, his authority and his family.' Lear loses his mind when he loses his social status. As the play progresses Lear is stripped of his 'conceptions of self'. He is forced to question his identity: 'Does any here know me?' … 'who is it that can tell me who I am?'

Dollimore believes that *King Lear* is really about 'power, property and inheritance', that Shakespeare is focusing on what happens when there is 'a catastrophic redistribution of power'. Society is 'torn apart by conflict' because of its 'faulty ideological structure'. Looking at the end of Act V Scene 3, Dollimore sees a total collapse. Edgar and Albany try vainly to 'recuperate their society in just those terms the play has subjected to sceptical interrogation'. Thus, for Dollimore, *King Lear* is a subversive, radical **tragedy** which questions the Jacobean status quo.

Leonard Tennenhouse, in his essay 'The Iconography of Power' (1986, reprinted in Kiernan Ryan ed. *King Lear: Contemporary Critical Essays*, 1993), refutes Dollimore's subversive reading. For him, *King Lear* shows us the opposite: the dangers of not following the 'old ways' of the patriarchal hierarchy. Tennenhouse would also deny that Shakespeare's portrayal of the sufferings of the poor and his concern with justice in *King Lear* are proof that the playwright viewed his society with a critical eye. However, other new historicist critics point to Lear's abuses of power as being direct comment on the vagaries of James I and his monarchy – so Shakespeare emerges as a social commentator.

## Feminist criticism

Feminist criticism can range from pointing out male prejudice in a text to arguing that women's experiences produce different ways of writing from men's. For Coppelia Kahn in 'The Absent Mother in *King Lear*' (1986, reprinted in Kiernan Ryan ed. *King Lear: Contemporary Critical Essays*, 1993), *King Lear* is a play about 'male anxiety'. Kahn suggests that Lear's breakdown occurs when he refuses to accept that he is dependent on his daughters. Lear goes mad because he cannot face his feminine side; he refuses to cry. When Lear learns to weep, and rediscovers a loving non-patriarchal relationship with Cordelia, he is redeemed. In Kahn's view the play affirms femininity as a positive force.

 **PROGRESS BOOSTER**

Critics' views are important because one of the best ways that we can inform and refine our responses is to compare them with the thinking of others. However, this does not mean that you can simply copy or repeat critics' views about the play as a substitute for engaging with it yourself. Examiners will still expect you to apply your intelligence to what you have read, reach your own conclusions and explain them in your own words.

Kathleen McCluskie's reading of *King Lear* in her essay 'The Patriarchal Bard' (1985, also reprinted in Ryan's 1993 collection) asserts the opposite view. For her, Lear is an 'anti-feminine' play. She suggests that the play shows female self-assertion and sexual desire as a source of evil, and male control of society as natural.

McCluskie points out that the play forces us to sympathise with the patriarchs, Lear and Gloucester, and the masculine power structure they represent. She does not feel that Shakespeare presents a movement towards the feminine in *King Lear*, rather the reverse: 'Family relations in this play are seen as fixed and determined, and any movement within them is portrayed as a destructive reversal of the rightful order.' For McCluskie, 'Cordelia's saving love, so much admired by critics, works … less as a redemption of womankind than as an example of patriarchy restored'. The audience is forced to agree that evil women (Goneril and Regan) create a chaotic world, and must be resisted. The feminine must either be made to submit (Cordelia) or destroyed (Goneril and Regan).

## Marxist criticism

A **Marxist** approach to criticism examines how literature has been shaped by the class structure and social changes of its period. Paul Delany offers a Marxist approach to *King Lear* in his essay '*King Lear* and the Decline of Feudalism' (1977, reprinted in Ivo Kamps ed. *Materialist Shakespeare*, 1995). He suggests that the **tragedy** is that of a traditional feudal society (represented by Lear and his subjects, who put great store in their beliefs and ceremonies) being challenged by a more modern outlook that is rational and individualistic and has no respect for their values (represented by Edmund, Goneril and Regan). In a sense this social change represents progress, but it also entails the destruction of much that is valuable.

## More recent critical approaches

A recent development from feminist analysis is one which examines the play's depiction of family relationships. Meredith Skura in her essay 'Dragon Fathers and Unnatural Children' (2008) asks whether, instead of interpreting Lear as a typical patriarchal male, we should look at him instead as a bad parent. Bruce Young in 'King Lear and the Calamity of Fatherhood' (2002) argues that the play presents a family situation in which father and daughters are all at fault to some degree and we should not necessarily take sides simply on the basis of gender.

The issue of poverty in today's world has led to consideration of vagrancy in the play. Michael Shurgot in his essay 'The Thing Itself' (1999) points out how the presence of the nearly naked Edgar in his role as Poor Tom suggests that all human beings, however high their social position, can suffer afflictions such as poverty and mental disturbance. Anthony Parr's chapter, 'The Wisdom of Nature' in Hiscock and Hopkins' *King Lear: A Critical Guide* (2011), offers the perspective of **ecocriticism**, reviewing the play's problematic depiction of nature in the light of modern environmental concerns.

To explore these diverse ideas further it is best to consider your own response to the play and then return to the critics themselves in full. You will find some of the critics mentioned here in the books listed in **Further reading.**

---

**KEY INTERPRETATION**  **A05**

Anthony Parr argues that, while a Marxist perspective may be useful when responding to the comments of Lear and Gloucester on social injustice, it is inadequate to the play as a whole: 'Marx theorised the economic order and relationships between classes but signally failed to reconceive the relationship between humanity and the natural world.' ('Ecological Perspectives in King Lear', in Hiscock and Hopkins eds. *King Lear: A Critical Guide*). In other words, by so thoroughly questioning what is natural and what unnatural, what is human and what animal, what is spiritual and what worldly, the play resists any single orthodox reading.

# PROGRESS CHECK

## Section One: Check your understanding

These tasks will help you to evaluate your knowledge and skills level in this particular area.

1. List three aspects of Shakespeare's plays that might be considered characteristic of the Renaissance.

2. Choose several scenes from *King Lear* and note, in the absence of scenery, what clues the audience would have about where each one is set.

3. Note three features of the play which are typical of the generation of playwrights to which Shakespeare belonged.

4. Draw a rough plan of the Globe stage and make notes on how a scene of your choice might be staged to appeal to an audience on three sides.

5. Write a paragraph discussing the major contrasts between the opening scene at court and the final scene at Dover.

6. Make notes on how the scenes set in Gloucester's residence show the shifting balance of power, and the immoral nature of Lear's opponents.

7. List the main faults found in *King Lear* by critics prior to the twentieth century.

8. Do you agree that comedy is an essential part of the play, as G. Wilson Knight suggests? Would the tragedy be less effective if it was removed? Write one to two paragraphs.

9. How convincing do you find the arguments for and against *King Lear* being a Christian play? Write a paragraph summarising your views.

10. How does Jonathan Dollimore's view of *King Lear* contrast with A. C. Bradley's? Write three or four bullet points.

## Section Two: Working towards the exam

Choose one of the following three tasks which require longer, more developed answers:

1. To what extent might the play be considered to challenge received ideas of gender?

2. 'For Lear the journey from his palace to Dover is a tragic fall, but for Edgar the same journey is a learning experience that prepares him for kingship.' Discuss.

3. 'Lear's identity is a social construction.' How far do you agree?

**A01  PROGRESS BOOSTER**

For each Section Two task, read the question carefully, select the key areas you need to address, and plan an essay of six to seven points. Write a first draft, giving yourself an hour to do so. Make sure you include supporting evidence for each point, including quotations.

| Progress check (rate your understanding on a level of 1 – low, to 5 – high) | 1 | 2 | 3 | 4 | 5 |
| --- | --- | --- | --- | --- | --- |
| The different ways that the play can be contextualised in its historical background | | | | | |
| How the conventions of the seventeenth-century theatre shaped the play's presentation | | | | | |
| How the settings of the play frame the unfolding of the plot | | | | | |
| The different interpretations of the play made by critics over time | | | | | |

## ASSESSMENT FOCUS

## How will you be assessed?

Each particular exam board and exam paper will be slightly different, so make sure you check with your teacher exactly which Assessment Objectives you need to focus on. You are likely to get more marks for Assessment Objectives 1, 2 and 3, but this does not mean you should discount 4 or 5. Bear in mind that if you are doing AS Level, although the weightings are the same, there will be no coursework element.

## What do the AOs actually mean?

| | Assessment Objective | Meaning? |
|---|---|---|
| **AO1** | Articulate informed, personal and creative responses to literary texts, using associated concepts and terminology, and coherent, accurate written expression. | You write about texts in accurate, clear and precise ways so that what you have to say is clear to the marker. You use literary terms (e.g. '**protagonist**') or refer to concepts (e.g. '**hamartia**') in relevant places – see **Genre: Tragedy**, page 75. You do not simply repeat what you have read or been told, but express your own ideas based on in-depth knowledge of the text and related issues. |
| **AO2** | Analyse ways in which meanings are shaped in literary texts. | You are able to explain in detail how the specific techniques and methods used by Shakespeare (e.g. recurrent **symbols**) influence and affect the reader's response. |
| **AO3** | Demonstrate understanding of the significance and influence of the contexts in which literary texts are written and received. | You can explain how *King Lear* might reflect the social, historical, political or personal backgrounds of Shakespeare or the time when it was written. You also consider how the play might have been received differently over time by audiences and readers. |
| **AO4** | Explore connections across literary texts. | You are able to explain links between *King Lear* and other texts, perhaps of a similar genre, or with similar concerns, or viewed from a similar perspective (e.g. **feminist**). |
| **AO5** | Explore literary texts informed by different interpretations. | You understand how the play can be viewed in different ways, and are able to write about these debates, forming your own opinion – for example, how one critic might view Kent as an embodiment of plain-speaking loyalty, whilst another might see him as a rigid spokesman for a snobbish hierarchy. |

## What does this mean for your revision?

Whether you are following an AS or A Level course, use the right-hand column above to measure how confidently you can address these objectives. Then focus your revision on those aspects you feel need most attention. Remember, throughout these Notes, the AOs are highlighted, so you can flick through and check them in that way.

Next, use the tables on page 91. These help you understand the differences between a satisfactory and an outstanding response. Then, use the guidance from page 92 onwards to help you address the key AOs, for example how to shape and plan your writing.

Features of **mid-level** responses: the following examples relate to the genre of **tragedy.**

| | Features | Examples |
|---|---|---|
| **A01** | You use critical vocabulary appropriately for most of the time, and your arguments are relevant to the task, ordered sensibly, with clear expression. You show detailed knowledge of the text. | *The opening scene shows Lear is* **at fault for the tragedy** *that follows. Other characters* **take advantage of the situation** *he creates, but it is his* **misjudgement** *in creating the 'love-test' and expelling Kent and Cordelia that* **gives evil its opportunity**. |
| **A02** | You show straightforward understanding of the writer's methods, such as how form, structure and language shape meanings. | *In Act III Scene 2 Lear enters* **shouting orders** *to the storm ('Blow … crack … rage! blow!'). This makes him seem a* **larger-than-life figure**, *yet it also* **makes clear** *just how self-centred and irrational he has become.* |
| **A03** | You can write about a range of contextual factors and make some relevant links between these and the task or text. | **Shakespeare's audience knew that a strong, wise ruler helped maintain order.** *They may have realised in this context that the rivalry between Albany and Cornwall mentioned in the first line is ominous, and they cannot have been surprised when Lear's irresponsible actions have results like a French invasion and deadly conflict between his daughters.* |
| **A04** | You consider straightforward connections between texts and write about them clearly and relevantly to the task. | *Gloucester seems almost as overwhelmed as* **Othello** *by the idea that someone he loves deeply has turned against him and,* **just like Othello***, in his emotional confusion he turns for guidance to the very person who is deceiving him. Edmund,* **like Iago***, is a* **Machiavel** *who looks for every opportunity to do damage.* |
| **A05** | You tackle the debate in the task in a clear, logical way, showing your understanding of different interpretations. | **Most critics seem to accept** *the Gentleman's view of Cordelia as a pure, innocent figure, yet* **it can be argued** *that through her original defiance of Lear and her invasion with a foreign army* **she contributes much to the tragedy**. |

Features of a **high-level** response: these examples relate to a task on narrative perspectives.

| | Features | Examples |
|---|---|---|
| **A01** | You are perceptive, and assured in your argument in relation to the task. You make fluent, confident use of literary concepts and terminology, and express yourself confidently. | *Cordelia's* **integrity** *is so firmly established by the support of Kent and France that when she denounces her sisters, we accept her word that their love is only, in her* **sharply dismissive adjective***, 'professed'.* |
| **A02** | You explore and analyse key aspects of Shakespeare's use of form, structure and language and evaluate perceptively how they shape meanings. | *By* **moving between plot and subplot***, Shakespeare is able to* **accelerate the consequences** *of each character's actions. Hardly, it seems, has Edmund betrayed his father than Gloucester is blinded, with Regan taunting Gloucester by saying that the son he once called 'natural' really 'hates' him.* |
| **A03** | You show deep, detailed and relevant understanding of how contextual factors link to the text or task. | *It is immediately clear that, as an* **illegitimate younger son***, Edmund has* **limited prospects***. His father 'acknowledges' him, but also sends him 'out' for nine years and intends to do so again. Many in the* **audience must have sympathised** *with his plight and felt some initial admiration for the cool way that he tricks his father and brother.* |
| **A04** | You show a detailed and perceptive understanding of issues raised, through connections between texts. You have a range of excellent supportive references. | **King Lear and Blanche in 'Streetcar'** *bear considerable guilt for the damage they do to themselves and others, yet as their stories unfold they* **move into the role of victim and finish as tragic scapegoats***, relatively innocent in comparison to those that abuse them.* |
| **A05** | You are able to use your knowledge of critical debates, and the possible perspectives on an issue to write fluently and confidently about how the text might be interpreted. | *Nature as addressed by Edmund (the law of the jungle) and as invoked by Lear (respect and kindness)* **seem to have nothing in common** *other than the name 'nature', yet the experiences which Edgar undergoes enable him to internalise both,* **ultimately unleashing the former to enforce the latter**. |

# HOW TO WRITE HIGH-QUALITY RESPONSES

The quality of your writing – how you express your ideas – is vital for getting a higher grade, and **AO1** and **AO2** are specifically about **how** you respond.

**EXAMINER'S TIP**

AO1 and AO2 are equally important in AS and A Level responses.

## Five key areas

The quality of your responses can be broken down into **five** key areas.

### 1. The structure of your answer/essay

- First, get **straight to the point in your opening paragraph.** Use a sharp, direct first sentence that deals with a key aspect and then follow up with evidence or detailed reference.
- **Put forward an argument or point of view** (you won't **always** be able to challenge or take issue with the essay question, but generally, where you can, you are more likely to write in an interesting way).
- **Signpost your ideas** with connectives and references which help the essay flow. Aim to present an overall argument or conceptual response to the task, not a series of unconnected points.
- **Don't repeat points already made,** not even in the conclusion, unless you have something new to add.

## Aiming high: Effective opening paragraphs

Let's imagine you have been asked the following question:

**'*King Lear* is a play about the corrupting effects of power?' To what extent do you agree?**

Here's an example of a successful opening paragraph:

| Gets straight to the point | The play starts with Lear abusing his power in the love test, a misdeed which damages him as well as others, leaving rivals to emerge and struggle for control of his kingdom. As their evil grows, Lear comes to see the dangers of any unrestrained authority, but it is far too late for him to set matters right. | Sets up some interesting ideas that will be tackled in subsequent paragraphs |

### 2. Use of titles, names, etc.

This is a simple, but important, tip to stay on the right side of the examiners.

- Make sure that you spell correctly the titles of the texts, authors and so on. Present them correctly too, with inverted commas and capitals as appropriate. For example, *In Act I of 'King Lear'* ….
- Use the **full title**, unless there is a good reason not to (e.g. it's very long).
- Use the term 'text' or 'play', rather than 'story'. If you use the word 'story', the examiner may think you mean the plot/action rather than the 'text' as a whole.

## 3. Effective quotations

Do not 'bolt on' quotations to the points you make. You will get some marks for including them, but examiners will not find your writing very fluent.

The best quotations are:

- Relevant and not too long (you are going to have to memorise them, so that will help you select shorter ones!)
- Integrated into your argument/sentence
- Linked to effect and implications

**EXAMINER'S TIP**

It's important to remember that *King Lear* is a text created by Shakespeare – thinking about the choices Shakespeare makes with language and plotting will not only alert you to his methods as a playwright but also his intentions, i.e. the effect he seeks to create.

## Aiming high: Effective use of quotations

Here is an example of an effective use of a quotation about suffering in the play:

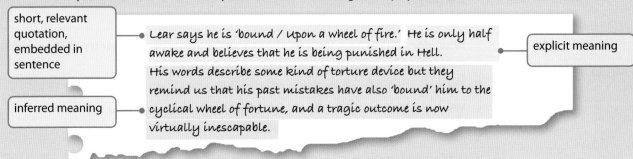

short, relevant quotation, embedded in sentence

inferred meaning

explicit meaning

Lear says he is 'bound / Upon a wheel of fire.' He is only half awake and believes that he is being punished in Hell. His words describe some kind of torture device but they remind us that his past mistakes have also 'bound' him to the cyclical wheel of fortune, and a tragic outcome is now virtually inescapable.

Remember – quotations can be one or two single words or phrases embedded in a sentence to build a picture or explanation, or they can be longer ones that are explored and picked apart.

## 4. Techniques and terminology

By all means mention literary terms, techniques, conventions, critical theories or people (for example, 'paradox', 'archetype', 'feminism' or 'Aristotle') **but** make sure that you:

- Understand what they mean
- Are able to link them to what you're saying
- Spell them correctly

## 5. General writing skills

Try to write in a way that sounds professional and uses standard English. This does not mean that your writing will lack personality – just that it will be authoritative.

- Avoid colloquial or everyday expressions such as 'got', 'alright', 'ok', and so on.
- Use terms such as 'convey', 'suggest', 'imply', 'infer' to explain the writer's methods.
- Refer to 'we' when discussing the audience/reader.
- Avoid assertions and generalisations; don't just state a general point of view (such as 'Edmund is a typical villain because he is evil'), but analyse closely with clear evidence and textual detail.

Note the professional approach here in the choice of vocabulary and awareness of the effect on the reader:

*Edmund has the typical qualities of a Machiavellian villain. He is discontented, cynical and self-serving, and able to disguise his villainous intentions behind a facade of honesty. However, his asides to the audience ensure that we are not deceived.*

**EXAMINER'S TIP**

Answer the question set, not the question you'd like to have been asked. Examiners say that often students will be set a question on one character (for example, the Fool) but end up writing almost as much about another (such as Lear). Or they write about one aspect of the question (for example, 'comic elements') but ignore another (such as 'tragedy'). **Stick to the question**, and answer **all parts of it**.

# QUESTIONS ABOUT A SPECIFIC EXTRACT

One type of question you may come across is one which asks you to consider a particular idea or aspect in relation to an extract from the play, and then widen the discussion to the play as a whole.

For example, you might be given this extract to write about:

> **Act IV Scene 1 lines 5–39, from 'The lamentable change' to 'Bless thee, master!'.**

Typical questions might relate to:

- The **dramatic significance** of the extract to the play as a whole, for example:

  **To what extent does this meeting of Gloucester and Edgar mark a turning point in the play?**

- A key **idea**, **issue** or **theme**:

  **What does this extract show us about how Gloucester and Edgar try to cope with misfortune?**

- The way a particular **character** or **relationship** is presented:

  **What kinds of change in the characters of Gloucester and Edgar, and in their relationship, does this extract suggest?**

It is important from your study that you are familiar with:

- **Who** is speaking, and what you know about them **at this stage in the play**

- **Where** and **when** the passage takes place in the text (Is it the ending of a scene or Act? What follows directly before and after it? Where does it take place?)

- What is **significant** about it: it is important you understand the extract's dramatic significance, even if that is not the main focus of the question

- How the **specific language** and **dramatic structure** enables us to understand more about the characters/relationships, ideas/issues or dramatic significance

So, for example, how might you explore the passage from Act IV Scene 1 as mentioned above, and what it tells us about how Gloucester and Edgar try to cope with misfortune? You might look at:

| Key questions to focus your reading and response | Possible answers | Effect (what it tells us about the key idea/issue) |
|---|---|---|
| Who is involved/speaking? What do we know about them? | *Gloucester and Edgar – they are estranged from one another and both have suffered due to Edmund's malice.* | *They reflect on their misfortunes and try to find some benefit, though it proves painfully hard to do so.* |
| Where and when does it take place? What has happened before this scene? | *Outside Gloucester's residence, after he has been blinded by Cornwall* | *Both characters are at their lowest point, but still seek to understand and do what is right.* |
| What is significant about the scene? | *Both are willing to take responsibility, Gloucester for his past errors, Edgar for his father's care.* | *Although Edgar does not reveal his identity, both men display a loyal, supportive attitude, which differentiates them from their enemies.* |
| What does the language and structure tell us? | *Gloucester's speech with the Old Man, and Edgar's asides, reveal their deepest feelings.* | *Edgar's initial optimism and Gloucester's failure to recognise his son show their fallibility, yet their reunion gives us some hope for their future.* |

# Writing a response

There are two key things you should do when writing about an extract, once you have 'done your thinking' along the lines suggested in the table:

- **Focus immediately** on **a specific aspect** from the scene; don't waste time with general waffle.
- **Develop your points** succinctly and swiftly but **using inference or insight** to explore them fully.

Here is an example of an excellent first paragraph:

> *In the first words spoken by Edgar in this extract, we see how he tries to cheer himself with the idea that once you have reached the 'worst', your fortune must improve and you can look forward to 'laughter', a conclusion cruelly undercut when he realises his father has been blinded. Edgar is forced to conclude that things can always get worse. From this point, we see him take matters into his own hands, not wait for fortune to help him.*

In subsequent paragraphs, there are two ways to proceed:

- Work through the extract in a straightforward linear fashion.
- Take your initial point and link it to a phrase, line, etc. later in the same extract.

If you take the latter route, your response may end up moving backwards and forwards within the passage, but it will allow you to make some interesting links. For example, you might want to take one particular aspect of the idea/issue being explored and trace one character's words, then move to another character.

For example:

> *Throughout the passage, Gloucester shows himself to be concerned for others. We see this in the exchange with the Old Man in lines 15–17, when he urges him to leave him in case trouble follows. His attitude is echoed by that of his son, who in his guise as Poor Tom shows his willingness to care for the father who so recently persecuted him.*

> **EXAMINER'S TIP**
>
> If you have a second question to answer once you have completed your detailed response to the passage, make sure you have left yourself enough time to write fully on the remaining task.

## Aiming high: Summarising events

Whilst it is important to understand the extract in terms of its plot significance, do not slip into simply retelling what has happened before and then telling the examiner what events are taking place now. Summarise important events swiftly and efficiently in a phrase or two, e.g. 'Following the blinding of Gloucester …'.

**EXAMINER'S TIP**

If you are following an AS course, you may have less time to write than for A Level – so concise, succinct points with less elaboration than provided here may be needed.

# GENERAL QUESTIONS ABOUT THE WHOLE TEXT

Such questions might be on a key issue or idea, or on the use of language or structure, for example: **'Does Shakespeare present a godless world in *King Lear*?'**

If you are tackling this question, you need to:

● Focus on **references** to pagan gods in the text and to Christian **interpretations** that seem to fit the play.

● Explain how Shakespeare **presents** or **organises** ideas about this.

● Look at the **whole text**, not just one scene or character.

● Consider **context** and **critical ideas**, e.g. engaging with the rival arguments that Lear achieves redemption through Cordelia and that the pagan setting is a way of showing a godless world while avoiding blasphemy.

## Structuring your response

You need a clear, logical plan, but it will be impossible to write about every aspect or section of the play. Start by noting down five or six key ideas:

*A: The play is set in pagan times and has many references to 'the gods'.*

*B: Lear's confidence in his divine right to rule proves to be misplaced.*

*C: Cordelia is a figure of redemption and Lear learns through suffering – both could have Christian implications.*

*D: Edgar and Albany praise divine justice, but Gloucester thinks humans are the gods' playthings.*

*E: Belief in the gods seems to aid morale; good triumphs in the end, though only at great cost.*

Then decide the most effective order for your points (e.g. D, B, A, C, E), and draw in supporting evidence and reference to context or critical ideas:

**Introduction:** *Many critics have argued that 'Lear' was a Christian play in which Jesus's redemption of humanity was figured by Cordelia's redemption of Lear. A more recent view is that the play is a sceptical one in which the characters struggle to find meaning in a godless universe. In order to evaluate these rival opinions, we must look closely at the evidence.*

**Paragraph 1 (point D):** *Shocked by news of Gloucester's blinding, Albany fears for the future of humanity if 'the heavens do not their visible spirits / Send quickly down' to punish the wicked. He is relieved to hear that Cornwall died carrying out his crime and declares, 'This shows you are above, / You justicers'. Edgar too claims that Gloucester's blinding is evidence that the 'Gods are just', but for the opposite reason, that his father deserved the punishment. Taken together these views seem to undermine one another, suggesting both men see divine justice only where it suits them.*

**Paragraph 2 (expand point D):** *The blinded Gloucester concludes, 'As flies to wanton boys, are we to th'Gods; / They kill us for their sport.' His view seems more deeply felt, but has no more authority than the others. As the play is set in a pagan era, the characters naturally express views which are not Christian in outlook.*

**Paragraph 3 (change to point B):** *Lear's view of the gods is more significant, since he is viewed by himself and others as the chief mortal representative of the divine order.*

... and so on.

**For your conclusion:** use a compelling way to finish, perhaps repeating words from the question. For example, you might end with a final point, but adding a last clause to clarify what you think is key to the answer:

*It is possible to interpret the world of the play as a godless universe, but also to see the play as a story about pagans which still endorses Christian values. Lear's is a world where cruelty and misfortune are all too common, but also one where love, conscience and a desire for justice may prevail, making Shakespeare's presentation more equivocal than sceptical.*

You could also end with a new aspect that is slightly different from your main point:

*'King Lear' is a play, not a sermon. It does not tell us about the world, but tells us a story about the world, leaving us to draw our own conclusions.*

# Writing about context

Depending on the course you are following, you may need to focus on aspects of context that are relevant to the area you are being asked to explore. **AO3** asks you to 'demonstrate understanding of the significance and influence of the contexts in which literary texts are written and received'. This can mean either of:

- How the events, settings, politics and so on **of the time when the text was written** influenced the writer or help us to understand the play's themes or concerns
- How events, settings, politics and so on **of the time when the text is read or seen** influence how it is understood

The table below will help you think about how particular aspects of the time in which the play was written contribute to our understanding now of the play and its themes, as related to the question on page 96.

the question on page 96.

> **EXAMINER'S TIP**
>
> Although understanding of contexts outside the play is very important, your work should ultimately arise **from the text itself**. You need to be able to explain and explore what the text seems to be saying about a particular social or political idea in parallel with what you know of the context in which it is written or received.

| Political | Literary | Philosophical |
|---|---|---|
| James I championed the divine right of kings, seeing himself (like Lear) as endorsed by a supernatural power, yet to many of his subjects he seemed a vain and corrupt ruler. | Earlier versions of the Lear story end with Lear restored to the throne and Cordelia alive. Did Shakespeare change this because he wanted to express a bleak view of life? | Atheism was loathed because it was assumed that a person with no belief in the supernatural would have no scruples about doing evil. Edmund is an example of this; so, perhaps, are Goneril, Regan and Cornwall. |
| **Scientific** | **Cultural** | **Social** |
| The growth of material knowledge suggested there might be alternative ways to explain human misbehaviour than labelling it 'sin'. Hence Lear asks, 'Is there any cause in nature that make these hard hearts?' | All plays were checked by the Masters of the Revels office. One feature to be censored was offensive religious references. If Shakespeare had wished to question religious belief, he would have had to do so obliquely. | All members of Shakespeare's audience would have been Christians. This would have made them especially sensitive to any religious issues or references. |

## Aiming high: Making context relevant

It is very important not to approach context as something to be 'bolted on' to what you say. You must make fluent links between contextual knowledge and the focus of the task. For example, **don't** just write:

*Although Shakespeare mentions no dates, the original King Lear is supposed to have reigned around the eighth century BC, before Britain had been Christianised. The characters in the play often mention 'gods' in the plural, showing that they worship several pagan deities. These include Hecate, goddess of witchcraft, and Apollo, the sun god.*

**Do** write:

*The play's pagan setting is made clear when Lear, offended by Cordelia's refusal to flatter him, swears his rejection of her by the sun and the 'mysteries of Hecate and the night'. His use of 'sacred' language demonstrates the seriousness of his intentions, but also shows us that he rules in the name of superstition.*

# QUESTIONS WITH STATEMENTS, QUOTATIONS OR VIEWPOINTS

You may come across questions which include a statement, quotation or viewpoint that offers a particular interpretation of the text. These might be in relation to the whole text or with regard to a specific extract, and may deal with character or key ideas. For example:

> **'Lear's painful journey towards clearer vision ultimately makes him admirable.'**
>
> **By considering Shakespeare's dramatic methods, to what extent do you agree with this view?**

The key thing to remember is that you are being asked to **respond to a particular perspective or critical view** of the text – in other words, to come up with **your own** 'take' on the idea or viewpoint in the task.

## Key skills required

The table below provides help and advice on answering the question above.

| Skill | Means? | How do I achieve this? |
|---|---|---|
| To consider different interpretations | There will be more than one way of looking at the given question. For example, critics might be divided about Lear's vision. Does he see the world more clearly or does he die confused and uncertain? | Show you have considered these different interpretations in your answer, through the way you juxtapose or weigh up ideas. For example: *We are relieved by Albany's declaration that Lear is confused as it spares him the pain of fully confronting the situation, yet the old king's priorities are unaffected. Cordelia remains everything to him.* |
| To write with a clear, personal voice | Your own 'take' on the question is made obvious to the examiner. You are not just repeating other people's ideas, but offering what you think. | Although you may mention different perspectives on the task, settle on your own view. Use language that shows careful, but confident, consideration. For example: *Although A. C. Bradley says of Lear, 'his nature was great', I do not find that the evidence supports this view. Lear admits his faults slowly and reluctantly, and ends the play a confused and pitiful figure.* |
| To construct a coherent argument | The examiner can follow your train of thought so that your own viewpoint is clear to him or her. | Write in clear paragraphs that deal logically with different aspects of the question. Support what you say with well-selected and relevant evidence. Use a range of connectives to help 'signpost' your argument. For example: *We might say that Lear never achieves total clarity of vision. However, the journey he undertakes is a heroic one. Moreover, as he loses his worldly power, he grows in spiritual stature.* |

## Responding to a 'viewpoint' question

Let us look at another question:

> **'Cordelia begins as a forceful, outspoken character but ends as a stereotype of female passivity.'**
>
> **To what extent do you agree with this view of Shakespeare's dramatic presentation of her?**

## Stage 1: Decode the question

Underline/highlight the **key words**, and make sure you understand what the statement, quote or viewpoint is saying. In this case:

'**To what extent do you agree ...**' means: *Do you agree totally with this statement or are there aspects of it you would dispute?*

'**stereotype of female passivity**' means: *a female character who does not defend herself and accepts her fate without complaining*

'**dramatic presentation of her**' means: *how her character is shown by the sequence of her actions and others' responses to them*

So you are being asked whether you agree/disagree with the view that Cordelia changes from a character who stands up for herself to one who does and says little and is only important for what is done to her.

## Stage 2: Decide what your viewpoint is

Examiners have stated that they tend to reward a strong view which is clearly put. Think about the question – can you take issue with it? Disagreeing strongly can lead to higher marks, provided you have **genuine evidence** to support your point of view. Don't disagree just for the sake of it.

## Stage 3: Decide how to structure your answer

Pick out the key points you wish to make, and decide on the order that you will present them in. Keep this basic plan to hand while you write your response.

## Stage 4: Write your response

Begin by expanding on the aspect or topic mentioned in the task title. In this way, you can set up the key ideas you will explore. For example:

*Cordelia begins the play as an assertive character, defying her father's expectations in the love-test, insisting her suitors receive a fair account of her and telling her sisters what she thinks of them. Later, she returns with an army to restore her father to the throne. Her final passivity only appears to be inconsistent.*

Then in the remaining paragraphs proceed to set out the different arguments or perspectives, including your own.

In the final paragraph, end with a clear statement of your viewpoint, but do not list or go over the points you have made. End succinctly and concisely.

> **EXAMINER'S TIP**
>
> You should comment concisely, professionally and thoughtfully and present a range of viewpoints. Try using modal verbs such as 'would', 'could', 'might', 'may' to clarify your own interpretation.

# USING CRITICAL INTERPRETATIONS AND PERSPECTIVES

## What is a critical interpretation?

The particular way a text is viewed or understood can be called an interpretation; it may be made by literary critics (specialists in studying literary texts), reviewers, or everyday readers and students. It is about taking a position on particular elements of the text, or on what others say about it:

### 1. Notions of 'character'

- Is the character an 'archetype' (a specific type of character with common features)? (For example, many people have commented that Lear begins as an archetypal figure of senior male authority, wrathful, unbending yet self-contradictory.)
- Does the character personify, **symbolise** or represent a specific idea (such as a self-contained individual, finally forced to realise that they depend upon others for consent, support and guidance)?
- Is the character modern, universal, of his/her time, historically accurate, etc? (For example, is Edmund the embodiment of modern ideas which subvert traditional precedence and order?)

### 2. Ideas and issues

This concerns what the play tells us about **particular ideas or issues** and how we interpret them, for example:

- Themes and ideas that obsessed Jacobean dramatists: the nature of good and evil; the difference between appearance and reality; corrupt authority figures
- The role of men/women in Jacobean society
- What **tragedy** means to Jacobean audiences
- Moral and social attitudes towards generational conflict

### 3. Links and contexts

This is how the play **links with, follows** or **pre-echoes** other texts or ideas, for example:

- Its influence culturally, historically and socially: Do we see echoes of the characters or genres in other texts such as *A Streetcar Named Desire* by Tennessee Williams or *A Thousand Acres* by Jane Smiley? How similar to other dominant father figures is Lear and why?
- How its language links to other texts or modes, such as religious works, myth, legend, etc.

### 4. Genre and dramatic structure

This is how the play is **constructed** and how Shakespeare **makes** his narrative:

- Does it follow a particular dramatic convention?
- What is the function of specific events, characters, theatrical devices, staging, etc. in relation to narrative?
- What are the specific moments of tension, conflict, crisis and **denouement** – and do we agree on what they are?

**EXAMINER'S TIP**

Critical interpretation of drama is of necessity different from critical interpretation of other modes of writing – not least because of audience response, and the specific theatrical devices in use. Key critics are theatre critics – look at what they have to say about recent productions. See the adjacent margin for just two examples of recent reviews of the 2014 National Theatre production of King Lear. These offer different 'readings' of the balance between the general scheme of the production and the dramatic power of the individual characters.

## 5. Audience and critical reaction

This covers how the play **works on an audience or reader**, and whether this changes over time and in different contexts. It also includes how different types of reader have responded, from reviewers, to actors and directors, to academics and researchers. For example:

- How far do readers or audiences empathise with, feel distance from, judge and/or evaluate the events and characters?
- What ideas do they find compelling and convincing, or lacking truth and impact?
- How far do they see the play as unique and modern, part of a tradition or carrying echoes of other works and ideas?

# Writing about critical perspectives

The important thing to remember is that **you** are a critic too. Your job is to evaluate what a critic or school of criticism has said about the elements above, arrive at your own conclusions, and also express your own ideas.

In essence, you need to: **consider** the views of others, **synthesise** them, then decide on **your perspective**.

### Explain the viewpoints

**Critical view A** about Edgar's tricking of his father:

> *John J. Norton believes Edgar leads his father through a therapeutic experience to draw him out of despair. Gloucester's suffering and 'redemption' parallel the fall and redemption of Lear.*

**Critical view B** about the same aspect:

> *R. A. Foakes asks whether Edgar is saving his father or playing 'another role, that of God'. Edgar's reluctance to tell his father who he is, his detachment from others and his readiness to explain away suffering leaves him a 'disturbing' character.*

### Then synthesise and add your perspective

> *Norton's view that Edgar is saving his father from despair is persuasive, given that this is where we see Edgar at last start to fight evil. However, at this stage Edgar is not so trusting or forgiving of his father that he will reveal his identity, so Foakes makes an equally convincing point in finding Edgar's behaviour disturbing in its detachment. In a tragedy where he is fated to fight his own brother to the death, Edgar is necessarily a complex, driven character.*

**EXAMINER'S TIP**

In *Time Out*, Andrzej Lukowski praised Adrian Scarborough's performance as 'a powerfully righteous Fool'. His acting was complemented by the staging, with black-clad soldiers conveying 'masculine menace' but still allowing room for the characters' relationships to grow. In *The New York Times*, Benn Brantley described Adrian Scarborough's excellence as the Fool more precisely: aware of his 'unsavory social role' he becomes 'more contemptuous and more charitable than anybody else'. However, Brantley felt that the excellent acting was eclipsed by the production: 'the spectacle would take over, as if by military force, and you could feel the production losing its emotional grip on the audience.'

# ANNOTATED SAMPLE ANSWERS

Below are extracts from three sample answers at different levels to the same task/question. Bear in mind that these responses may not correspond exactly to the style of question you might face, but they will give a broad indication of some of the key skills required.

> **Read from Act II Scene 4: 'Lear: Is this well spoken?' to 'O fool I shall go mad!'**
>
> **By analysing Shakespeare's dramatic methods, explore the significance of the extract to the tragedy of the play as a whole.**

## Candidate 1

The extract takes place at Gloucester's castle. Goneril has been showing Lear disrespect. She refuses to allow him all his hundred followers, so he decides he will stay with her sister Regan. Goneril warns Regan that Lear is coming, so she and Cornwall visit Gloucester. When Lear arrives at Gloucester's, chasing her, we can see that he is not a proper king any more, but has to chase after his daughters for somewhere to live. The audience sees him lose his dignity, especially once he finds that Regan's husband Cornwall has actually put his messenger in the stocks. This is a punishment of the king's messenger which shows no respect for the king either. Lear can't make anyone do anything any more, as he could when he was a proper king. He has to argue about keeping his hundred followers. The way we see Lear in this situation, contrasting with the way he commanded everyone in Act I Scene 1, makes it obvious that he is having a tragic fall. By the end of the extract, he has been brought to tears and has run away, with the symptoms of a nervous breakdown.

When Lear asks, 'Is this well-spoken?' it shows us that he cannot believe what he is hearing. Regan has suggested to him that he goes back to Goneril and she has made it clear that she sympathises with her sister, not with him. She tries to reason with him, making her points through questions, but taking care to answer them herself to head off his replies. The effect on the audience is to show us that she knows the answers she wants to hear and that's all she will accept. Goneril joins in and encourages Regan, showing us that the two daughters are now ganging up on their father.

Lear does not speak for thirteen whole lines. This suggests that he is speechless with shock and anger at the way he is being treated by the daughters he brought up and gave so much to. When Regan suggests twenty-five followers might be enough for him, he says to her, 'I gave you all'. Lear may have behaved wrongly towards his daughters, but we can see from what he says and how hurt he is that it is unjust for them to treat him in this way. Regan says to him, 'And in good time you gave it.' This shows us the frustration she must have felt while waiting to inherit. The effect is to make us feel there is a history of unspoken issues in this royal family, to do with inheritance, respect and favouritism, and we are seeing it finally erupt into the open.

**Annotations:**

- **A01** Too much story summary, rather than analysis
- **A02** Explains effect of what we see on stage
- **A01** Reference to an additional scene, linked to tragedy genre
- **A02** Perceptive point; could support analysis with term 'rhetorical question'
- **A02** Perceptive comment; could emphasise method and effect
- **A03** Useful interpretation, linked to contextual issues; could be more developed

Later in the play, the worst jealousy will turn out to be the jealousy between the two sisters themselves, not between them and Lear. We see this in their rivalry over Edmund which leads to Goneril poisoning Regan.

> **A04** Reference to later developments contextualises the extract

Lear gets nowhere with Regan, so he turns back to Goneril and decides to accept her offer of fifty followers. The effect of this is to show us how poor his judgement is. He seems to have been a king for so long that he has no understanding of anything except being obeyed. It is obvious to the audience that Goneril is just going to lower her offer to match Regan's. The truth turns out to be even worse, as the two women agree that he needs no followers at all. Instead, he can rely on their servants. When we think of Goneril's henchman Oswald, and the way that the daughters treat Gloucester once they have taken control of his house, ordering him about, then blinding him, we can see that Lear is more likely to be treated as a prisoner than a guest.

> **A02** Strong point that would be improved by use of the term 'dramatic irony'

He tries to reason with his daughters, arguing that they are only talking about his physical needs as though he was an animal. He also has the needs of a human being, like respect. His argument is interrupted by his tears, showing us that he is overcome by his emotions. After losing control of Britain and his family, he is now losing control of himself. Trying to be angry rather than upset, he makes vague threats ('I will do such things, / What they are, yet I know not, but they shall be / The terrors of the earth'). But he cannot hold his tears back, so he runs out of the house, crying out to the Fool that he is afraid he will go mad. It seems that the way he has been treated by his daughters has proved too much for his mind. He used to be their father and king. Now they no longer respect him.

> **A02** Excellent summary of the overall effect

The overall effect of the scene is that it shows us Lear's defeat by his daughters and it also explains why he becomes mentally disturbed. We are prepared for his later obsessions with Goneril and Regan, also with human nature and the ways people abuse authority. Eventually he comes to realise that his own behaviour has not been all it should be and I believe that he learns through his tragic suffering.

> **A01** Significance of extract explained, but would be clearer if supported by more specific examples

> **A05** Personal response shown, but little engagement with alternative interpretations

## MID LEVEL

**Comment**

- The points are convincing and are made clearly.
- There is a tight focus on the effects and significance of the extract, with some useful, if limited references, to other parts of the play.
- Expression is clear, though sometimes unsophisticated.

**To improve the answer:**

- Begin to answer from the very start; don't waste time on excessive plot summary. (AO1)
- Ensure points are linked explicitly to the question and supported by literary terms. (AO1)
- Make more detailed references to other parts of the play. (AO4)
- Keep quotations brief. (AO1)

## Candidate 2

**A01** A firm point is made in the first sentence and linked to the tragic genre

The extract is an important one as it is a decisive moment in Lear's tragic descent from all-powerful ruler to homeless and broken old man. There is a strong contrast between the way Regan spoke to Lear in the love-test, when she claimed that her father's love was her only happiness and that she was 'an enemy to all other joys', and the tone she takes with him now that she has the upper hand. Because Goneril has gone back on her pledge to let him have a hundred followers, Lear has pursued Regan to Gloucester's castle to ask her to take him in, but she is determined to keep in step with her sister. She tells Lear, 'being weak, seem so'. When he reminds her that he gave her everything, she snaps, 'And in good time you gave it.' There is no gratitude in her voice and no willingness to put herself out to help him. She called him 'your dear highness' in the opening scene, when she was hoping to get land and riches from him. Now it is just, 'my Lord'. The effect of these changes is to show us how much power Lear has lost. We see what Regan and Goneril really think of him.

**A01** Insightful reference to l.1

**A02** Convincing analysis of methods and effects, well supported by short quotations

In the love-test the two elder daughters had to compete with each other and with Cordelia. Now we see them standing side by side, questioning Lear as though he was in the dock (they ask him eight questions during the extract, all of them rhetorical). They tell him that his followers will disrupt their peace and he ought to rely on their staff instead. They 'have a command to tend you', but this command will come from the daughters, not from Lear, and remain theirs to take back. It seems that Lear does not fully understand how his relationship with his daughters has changed. He says that Goneril must love him twice as much as Regan because she has previously said she would allow him twenty-five followers. He is soon corrected in his mistake, as both daughters insist that he gets rid of all his knights, slyly disguising their insistence as mere questions for him to consider ('What need one?'). To take away a king's courtly entourage is to take away his independence for good and put him totally in their power.

**A02** Reference to positioning of actors on stage, though method/effect analysis should be more explicit

**A03** Good contextual point

**A01** Another insightful reference to l.1, but again relevance to the question needs to be made explicit

Unable to tell them what to do any more, Lear tries to argue back, which to his daughters and to the audience is a further sign of his weakness. He gets not a word of support from the Fool or Gloucester, who do not dare intervene in such a dispute between members of the royal family. There is no Earl of Kent this time to butt in and speak up for common sense. The effect of this is to show us that the king is isolated.

Lear tries to convince Regan and Goneril that it is not proper to argue about his 'need' for supporters, because assessing a person on their needs without taking account of their wants is the same as treating them like an animal. He breaks off this argument, overcome by tears.

**A01** Another helpful link between the extract and I.1

He is afraid of showing how powerless he is, so he starts to call upon the gods and begs them to give him 'noble anger'. When he swore by the gods in the first scene of the play, it seemed to scare the court, but this time no one is impressed. Since his attempt to call upon the heavens does not work, he tries to threaten his daughters, but he cannot think of any 'terrors' he could inflict on them and is reduced to running out of the castle in tears. This shows us that he has lost his sense of kingship, fatherhood and manhood. Lear is scared he can no longer cope with the pressure of reality and he exclaims, 'O Fool! I shall go mad.'

**A05** Clear summary and thorough approach to the debate

**A01** Concluding paragraph addresses the question firmly

The extract is a turning point for two main reasons. Firstly, it makes clear the cruelty of Goneril and Regan. Having finally overthrown their father, they gain in confidence and will soon do evil to Gloucester. Secondly, the extract show us Lear's tragic transformation from king to madman. For most of Acts III and IV he will brood on what has happened and why. At times he returns to his failed threats, trying to put Regan and Goneril through an imaginary trial, at others he questions the political system that he used to head. Now he can see it has left 'poor naked wretches' to suffer poverty and exposure to the elements. He realises he had been misled into thinking he was wise and invulnerable ('ague-proof'), that he was a figure of natural authority. Now he sees 'They flattered me like a dog'. He accepts that he has become a 'fond, foolish old man' and makes his peace with Cordelia. Cordelia does not see Lear as a dangerous nuisance, but as a vulnerable parent who should be cared for respectfully. She calls him 'royal Lord' and 'your Highness'. The extract is also important, therefore, as a reference point for how the king is treated.

**A04** Awareness of tragedy genre and its progression through the play – could be more developed

**A01** Quotations need more explanation to be fully effective

**A02** Perceptive analysis of method and effect, though it would benefit from more explanation

GOOD LEVEL

**Comment**

- A clear, coherent argument, giving a thorough account of the extract.
- Some helpful, quite detailed references to earlier and later scenes.
- Analysis is convincing.
- Expression is clear and concise, with some use of literary terms.

**To improve the answer:**

- Make sure points are always explicitly linked to the question. (AO1)
- Explain dramatic effects and examples more fully. (AO2)
- Add an explicit conclusion. (AO1)

## Candidate 3

**A01** Scene immediately put into context

This is the crucial moment in the play, when Lear is stripped of control, contrasting with the opening scene when he seemed almost god-like as he divided up the country and dismissed Cordelia and Kent from the court. Having demonstrated to his daughters how royal power can be abused, he becomes a victim in turn, though their treatment of him is comparatively subtle and manipulative. Lear seems less equipped to cope than his own victims, more dangerously dependent on his courtly role for his sense of identity, and in this lies much of his tragedy.

**A01** Several sophisticated links made to I.1

Lear had made it clear that he intended his elder daughters' power to have limits. They are supposed to be his 'guardians', looking after his affairs on his behalf, and to have accepted that he will retain a stated number of followers. Lear reiterates these conditions in exasperation, as though trying to convince himself that the problem lies in his daughters' lack of understanding, but as the Fool in his role of chorus has repeatedly made clear to us, Lear has effectively enthroned Goneril and Regan. The more he is forced to argue about the details of the settlement, the more evident it becomes to us that he has now lost control over his own fate.

**A01** Excellent use of a literary term to convey Shakespeare's dramatic method

**A01** Insightful reference to later developments

Lear's hope that he can play off the two women against one another is not ill founded, as their later rivalry over Edmund makes clear. At this stage, however, they are determined to 'hit together'. Literally standing shoulder to shoulder, they take it in turns to talk down the number of his followers, using a series of what are effectively rhetorical questions to force him to concur ('Why not, my Lord?'). Their pretence of spontaneity ('now I spy a danger') scarcely conceals their shared intention. Regan's vocabulary ('danger ... commands ... control') shows us her domineering mentality.

**A02** Confident use of quotation

**A02** Perceptive remarks on language as a dramatic method

**A02** Interruption of one character by another as a dramatic method

With his followers reduced from a hundred to a proposed twenty-five, Lear cries out in anguish, 'I gave you all', only to be interrupted (itself a sign of disrespect) by Regan's scathing comment, 'And in good time you gave it.' If we have had some provisional sympathy for Goneril and Regan, this is the point where we realise just how selfish and ruthless the two daughters are.

**A03** Excellent linking of genre and context

While our sympathy for Lear grows in proportion to our dislike for them, the fact that he remains in denial about his plight shows us that he is unable to see himself in any role other than king – his very kingliness could be seen as his tragic flaw, as Lear's refusal to loosen his grip on feudal power is linked to his downfall. His calculation that Goneril loves him twice as much as Regan because she might permit him fifty followers shows us he has not outgrown the mind-set of the love-test. There is a degree of dramatic irony here; if Lear does not realise that Goneril's offer will lapse, we certainly do. Her question 'What need you five-and-twenty, ten, or five?' confirms our suspicion and is capped by Regan's, 'What need one?', the effect of which is to mark for us the end of Lear's power.

**A02** Sophisticated analysis of dramatic method

He responds with a speech which starts with rational argument and ends in despair. As he is forced to realise his true position, Lear breaks down before our eyes; his speech acts out the process. He fails to complete his initial argument, that human nature has more requirements than the basic necessities for survival. Perhaps he cannot face the indignity of explaining his own dependence. Halted by a surge of emotion, he reverts desperately to his habits of divine right, calling on the 'Heavens' and the 'Gods' to prevent him from crying. If he can manifest 'noble anger', he will be able to retain at least something of his self-esteem. Instead he responds with tears, 'women's weapons', a reversal which he feels to be 'unnatural' and unbearable.

**A02** Effective use of brief quotations

Lear resorts to pitiful threats, which he cannot explain, let alone carry through. His incoherence and the sobs which he refuses to acknowledge to be weeping present us with a man far removed from the figure of authority who headed the procession of nobles at the beginning of the play. As he flees his daughters' presence, with the sound of a distant storm echoing the breakdown of the old order, he has no one to turn to now but the Fool, and nowhere to go but the exposed countryside.

**A02** Good reference to sound effects as a dramatic method, though more could be written about how this prepares us for the next scene

**A03** Detailed knowledge of how the extract fits into the whole play, in terms of contrasting settings

This expulsion is permanent. He may sometimes be at court in his imagination, but a heath, a hovel, an outhouse and the countryside near Dover are the inhospitable settings occupied by Lear until his death at Albany's encampment. From his new perspective away from the court, and with his normal habits of thought dissolved in 'madness', Lear comes to see himself and the nature of power more clearly and to rethink his values. Once he was flattered to be told by Kent that he had natural authority; now he tells Gloucester that authority depends only on social position: 'A dog's obeyed in office.' In contrast to his confrontation with Goneril and Regan, he embraces Cordelia and rejoices at his reunion with her, scorning the passing chatter of 'court news'. His understanding of the inauthenticity of the system he once represented raises Lear's downfall from misfortune to tragedy, and it follows from his dramatic loss of power and status in Act II Scene 4.

**A04** Excellent reference creating links across the text, with a supporting quotation

**A05** Conclusion shows the confident and perceptive response to the task employed throughout

**VERY HIGH LEVEL**

**Comment**

- Writing is assured, fluent and perceptive.
- The argument ranges freely across the text to place the extract in context and bring out its significance.
- Points are highly perceptive, with a range of dramatic methods noted and analysed.

# PRACTICE TASK

Now it's your turn to work through an exam-style task on *King Lear*. The key is to:

- Quickly read and decode the task/question
- Briefly plan your points – then add a few more details, such as evidence, or make links between them
- Write your answer

## Decode the question

> 'The main impression left on the audience at the end of King Lear is that after all the suffering there is little consolation.'
>
> By considering Shakespeare's dramatic methods, to what extent do you agree with this view?

| | |
|---|---|
| 'main impression' | suggests that you should focus on the dominant effect of the play, not subsidiary elements like comic relief |
| 'suffering' | suggests that you need to take clear account of the most tragic features, such as Gloucester's blinding and Cordelia's hanging |
| 'little consolation' | suggests that you must examine positive elements and assess their effect in proportion to the tragic features |
| 'dramatic methods' | suggests you must focus on what Shakespeare does – though not just language, but also structuring of events, for example. |
| 'to what extent do you agree?' | What is your view? Do you agree with the statement completely, partially or not at all? |

## Plan and write

- Decide your viewpoint
- Plan your points
- Think of key evidence and quotations (look again at Act V Scene 3)
- Write your answer

### EXAMINER'S TIP

Remember to incorporate the views of critics, but make sure that the central idea is your own. For example: *Critic Jan Kott suggested that 'King Lear' is 'a morality play in which everyone will be destroyed'. Although the play does show characters and their beliefs tested to destruction, I think Anthony Parr's argument that the play is questioning our sense of human needs is a far more compelling approach.'*

### Success criteria

- Show your understanding of the two key ideas as aspects of tragedy
- Draw on a range of critical views or different interpretation as appropriate
- Sustain your focus on the ideas of 'suffering' and 'consolation'
- Argue your point of view clearly and logically
- Make perceptive points and express your ideas confidently
- Support your points with relevant, well-chosen evidence, including quotations
- Use literary terminology accurately and appropriately with reference to the effect on the reader
- Write in fluent, controlled and accurate English

Once you have finished, use the **Mark scheme** on page 120 to evaluate your response.

## FURTHER READING

### The text and its sources

Frank Green, ed., *King Lear*, Heinemann Advanced Shakespeare, Heinemann 2000

This is the edition of the text used in the preparation of these Notes. It includes helpful notes on the text and many study activities

R. A. Foakes, ed., *King Lear*, The Arden Shakespeare, Thomson Learning, 1997

The Arden edition includes scholarly annotations and a fine and comprehensive introduction to the play

Jay L. Halio, ed., *The Tragedy of King Lear*, Cambridge University Press, 2005

A scholarly edition of the Folio text, with excellent introduction and notes, and detailed discussion of how the Folio and Quarto texts differ

Kenneth Muir, ed., *King Lear: Penguin Critical Studies*, Penguin, 1986

For a full discussion of Shakespeare's sources for *King Lear*, the section called 'The Making of the Play' is excellent.

Gary Taylor and Stanley Wells, eds, *The Complete Works*, Clarendon Press, 1986

The Quarto and Folio texts of King Lear are printed separately and the editors provide a detailed discussion of their histories. There is also a compact edition of *The Complete Works*, published in 1988

### Criticism

This list represents a very small tip of an enormous critical iceberg. Collections of criticism are very useful since they provide a range of views of the play. Some of the best recent collections include:

Susan Bruce, ed., *Shakespeare – King Lear*, (Readers' Guides to Essential Criticism), Palgrave Macmillan, 1999

Traces the development of critical debates about the play, and the ways in which the play has been evaluated and re-evaluated. There are extracts from critics from several centuries

John Drakakis, ed., *Shakespearean Tragedy*, Longman, 1992

A selection of contemporary views. There are four essays specifically about *King Lear*. In the introduction Drakakis provides a detailed summary of views about tragedy, which is particularly helpful for undergraduates. The Dollimore essay is reprinted here

Andrew Hiscock and Lisa Hopkins, eds., *King Lear: A Critical Guide*, Continuum, 2011

A very helpful review of critical debates and resources, which includes Anthony Parr's essay on ecocriticism

Frank Kermode, Ed., *King Lear: A Casebook*, Macmillan, 1992

This collection covers a range of criticism of *King Lear*, including the views of some of the play's early critics

Frank Kermode, *Shakespeare's Language*, Allen Lane The Penguin Press, London, 2000

A masterful, perceptive discussion of how Shakespeare's language achieves its effects, containing a valuable chapter on *King Lear*

Kiernan Ryan, ed., *King Lear: A Casebook*, New Casebooks, Macmillan, 1993

An excellent selection of recent views. Four critics referred to in the section on **Critical history** – Dollimore, Tennenhouse, Kahn, McCluskie – can be found here.

Other well-known critics who are worth reading on *King Lear*:

Harold Bloom ed., *King Lear*, (Bloom's Reviews: Comprehensive Research and Study Guides), Chelsea House Publishers, 1999

A. C. Bradley, *Shakespearean Tragedy*, 3rd edition, ed. by J.R. Brown, Macmillan, 1992

An influential critic from the beginning of the twentieth century, Bradley focuses on character and motivation

W. R. Elton, *King Lear and the Gods*, San Marino, California, 1966

A full discussion of religion and religious attitudes in the play

Rex Gibson, *Shakespearean and Jacobean Tragedy*, (Cambridge Contexts in Literature), Cambridge University Press, 2001

Explores literary, historical and social contexts

Harley Granville-Barker, *Prefaces to Shakespeare II*, London, 1927, reissued in 1982

As a playwright and director, Granville-Barker provides useful insight into staging Shakespeare's plays

Jan Kott, *Shakespeare Our Contemporary*, Cambridge University Press, 1964

Provides a bleak, existentialist reading of the view of humanity portrayed in the play

Alistair McCallum, *King Lear*, (The Shakespeare Handbooks), Ivan R. Dee Inc, 2001

Claire McEachern, *The Cambridge Companion to Shakespearean Tragedy*, Cambridge University Press, 2003

John Russell Brown, *Shakespeare: The Tragedies*, Palgrave, 2001

There are two chapters on the play, covering themes, characters and the two plots

Kiernan Ryan ed., *Shakespeare: Texts and Contexts*, Macmillan, 2000

There is an excellent chapter on the play by Graham Martin and Stephen Regan, who consider *King Lear* from a variety of angles in an accessible way. There are sections on the plot, the double plot, themes, characters, madness, nature, power and morality, the historical context of the play, religious interpretations of the play, gender and performance. Also includes images of some productions. Highly recommended

Gamini Salgado, *King Lear: Text and Performance*, Macmillan, 1993

Topics covered include the world of the play, dramatic style and structure, conceptions of character and relationships, settings and costumes

G. Wilson Knight, *The Wheel of Fire*, 4th edition, Routledge, 1989

Includes two fine essays, '*King Lear* and the Comedy of the Grotesque' and 'The *Lear* Universe'

### Shakespeare's Life and Theatre

Samuel Schoenbaum, *Shakespeare: A Documentary Life*, Oxford University Press, 1975

Andrew Gurr, *The Shakespearean Stage*, Cambridge University Press, 1992

Invaluable for anyone interested in the history of the Elizabethan playhouses, staging practices and acting companies

# LITERARY TERMS

**absurd** a view of life in which the universe is indifferent and incomprehensible, human existence is characterised by anxiety, and all human action is ineffectual and ridiculous – a view explored by some novelists and dramatists in the years after the Second World War

**aside** a common dramatic convention in which a character speaks in such a way that some of the characters on stage do not hear what is said. It may also be a direct address to the audience, revealing the character's views, thoughts, motives and intentions

**blank verse** unrhymed iambic pentameter: each line contains five stresses, normally falling on the even syllables

**chorus** in the tragedies of the ancient Greek playwrights, the 'chorus' is a group of characters who represent the ordinary people and who comment on the action. The Fool is in some ways a choral character: he is not a major participant in the events witnessed, but his comments are full of ironic insight

**denouement** the final unfolding of a plot: the point at which the reader's expectations, be they hopes or fears, about what will happen to the characters are finally satisfied or denied

**dramatic irony** a feature of many plays: it occurs when the development of the plot allows the audience to possess more information about what is happening than some of the characters have

**ecocriticism** an examination of the ways literature represents the relationship between human beings and nature

**feminism** in literature, an attempt to explore or expose the masculine 'bias' in texts and challenge traditional ideas about them, offering an alternative perspective

**foil** a character who can be contrasted with and compared to a more major one

**imagery** the figurative language in a piece of literature (metaphors and similes); or all the words that refer to objects and qualities which appeal to the senses and feelings

**irony** saying or writing one thing while meaning another, with the true meaning contradicting the surface one to some degree

**Machiavellian** the Machiavel was a villainous stock character in Elizabethan and Jacobean drama, so called after the Florentine writer Niccolo Machiavelli (1469–1527), who recommended to rulers that under certain circumstances they should lie to the populace for their own good and to preserve power. In drama, Machiavels are practised liars and cruel opportunists, who delight in their own manipulative evil

**Marxism** Marxist studies examine how literature has been shaped by class structure and social change. Recent critics often have reservations about traditional Marxism, so pursue a modified version of this approach under the name 'cultural materialism'

**metaphor** a strong form of comparison in which one thing is described as though it was another

**new historicism** a discussion of literary works in terms of their place in a wider cultural history

**paradox** an apparently self-contradictory statement, which nonetheless contains some meaning or truth

**pathos** strong feelings of pity aroused by a literary episode

**plot** the 'plan' of a literary work, creating a pattern of relationships between events. More loosely, it may refer to separate narratives within one larger story. Elizabethan and Jacobean drama commonly features a **main plot** and a **subplot**

**poetic justice** the idea that literature should always depict a world in which virtue and vice are eventually judged and appropriately rewarded and punished

**soliloquy** a direct speech to the audience, as if the character is thinking aloud about motives, feelings and decisions. By giving accurate access to the character's innermost thoughts, it enables us to learn more about the character than could ever be gathered from the action of the play alone

**symbol** something which represents something else. Many symbols are traditional, e.g. the dragon (I.1.121) is an emblem of the ancient British monarchy. Writers also develop their own symbols, something using them as a kind of recurrent metaphor, e.g. a storm in Shakespeare's writings often stands for a time of misfortune which shows us a character's innermost nature through the way they respond

**tragedy** a play which traces the downfall of an individual, and shows in so doing both the capacities and limitations of human life

# REVISION TASK ANSWERS

## Revision task 1: Changing characters

Make notes on which characters have changed in the first Act and in what ways. Write about:

– Changes in their position and status

– Changes in their personality

- Lear starts the play as a forceful, seemingly confident king, but after handing over his powers to Goneril and Regan he becomes little more than Goneril's slighted house guest and the butt of the Fool's humour – he grows ill-tempered, increasingly ineffectual and even fearful for his sanity.
- Goneril initially flatters her father due to her dependency on him, but having gained power she plots against him with her sister and Oswald, firmly tells Lear off and grows ever more domineering.
- Kent is a leading figure at the court who speaks his mind to Lear – banished, he reappears in the guise of a lowly servant, but continues to speak and behave forcefully.
- Gloucester is a respected earl who loves both of his sons – taken in by Edmund's lies, he proves an easy dupe and is filled with ill-judged anger towards Edgar.
- Edgar begins the play as heir to the earldom of Gloucester, but his status and security are destroyed by Edmund's trickery.

## Revision task 2: Loyalty and disloyalty

Cornwall tells Edmund, 'you shall be ours' (line 113) and Edmund replies, 'I shall serve you, Sir' (line 115). Make notes on:

– Which characters owe allegiance to others

– Whether in your view they serve them loyally or let them down

- Kent tries hard to serve his king, even risking death by secretly returning from banishment – but it is possible that his assertive behaviour makes things worse rather than better.
- Oswald is Goneril's steward and carries out all her instructions – unlike Kent, he never offers unpopular advice or questions the wisdom and morality of his orders.
- Edmund should owe allegiance to the father who publicly acknowledges him and has paid for his upbringing, but instead he despises Gloucester and schemes to succeed to his title.
- Cordelia accepts that she is beholden to her father ('you have begot me, bred me, loved me', I.1.95) and, presumably, defies him in the love-test merely to shock him into his senses – yet she embarrasses him in front of the court and her actions have the disastrous result that Goneril and Regan take over the whole kingdom.
- Regan and Goneril owe allegiance to Lear, but their flattering words in the love-test are hollow and they soon plot to 'hit together' (I.1.302–3) against him.

## Revision task 3: The wisdom of fools

It is common in Shakespeare's plays for the greatest wisdom to come from characters who seem very foolish. Kent points out to Lear that his Fool's songs and jokes contain many perceptive comments: 'This is not altogether Fool, my Lord' (I.4.149). Sometimes an extreme state of mind or unorthodox point of view allows the characters to realise truths that others prefer not to notice.

Find examples of characters in the play whom others might class as mad or disturbed and note what truths they are able to express as a result of their unusual point of view.

- Lear declares, 'they told me I was every thing; 'tis a lie, I am not ague-proof' (IV.6.105) – his experience of suffering, epitomised by the storm on the heath, shows him that a king is not necessarily wiser or less vulnerable to fate than an ordinary person.
- Lear calls a dog barking at a beggar the 'great image of Authority' (IV.6.156) – he sees that authority such as he once had is gained not merely by one's personal qualities, but by one's place in a power structure.
- Mourning over Cordelia's dead body, Lear says, 'Thou'lt come no more' (V.3.307) – even as he himself is dying, he realises that life is precious and should be used wisely.
- Pretending to be Poor Tom, Edgar speaks of sin in animal terms: 'hog in sloth, fox in stealth, wolf in greediness, dog in madness, lion in prey' (III.4.94–5) – implying that a human being should rise above his animal instincts and act with wisdom and intelligence.
- Even when suicidal due to his torture and shame, Gloucester's deepest prayer is 'If Edgar live, O, bless him!' (IV.6.40) – he realises his love for his elder son is the most important thing in his life.

## Revision task 4: Does Lear remain at the play's centre?

'By the end of Act IV, the focus of the drama has switched from Lear to Edgar.'

How far do you agree with this statement? List as many reasons for and against it as you can.

- Edgar looks after Gloucester and kills Oswald when he tries to murder him – by doing so, he emerges as a champion of good against evil.
- Edgar has a letter proving Goneril and Edmund are conspiring to murder Albany – with this evidence he has a good chance of at last overcoming his brother.
- Lear, meanwhile, has been reduced to the passive role of invalid, at first wandering the countryside, later being looked after by Cordelia.
- Nonetheless, the play devotes more attention to Lear's story than Edgar's, so that Lear remains the more central character.
- Lear has the status and significance of a king who has been overthrown but who may yet be reinstated – we do not realise until the end of the play that Edgar will be the next ruler.

## Revision task 5: Conflict among the usurpers

Goneril, Regan and Edmund, along with their reluctant ally Albany, are challenged by people loyal to Lear and by their own internal divisions.

Make notes on what each of them wants and how this turns them against one another.

- Regan desires to marry Edmund and take power with him, but her sister is her rival for his love and so becomes her enemy.

- Goneril also desires to marry Edmund and take power with him – in order to be in a position to do so, she plans to kill her sister and her own husband Albany.
- Edmund is secretly engaged to both Regan and Goneril, so cannot take power unless one of them dies – he will also need to dispose of Albany.
- Goneril and Regan are the older sisters, so they should be able to claim royal priority over Cordelia and debar Lear as incapable of ruling – but Edmund needs to kill Lear and Cordelia in order to stake his claim to the throne.
- Edmund also needs to eliminate his older brother and seems to assume he has already done so – a major error.

## Revision task 6: The depiction of women

'The play offers us only simple female stereotypes: the saintly Cordelia and her two wicked sisters.'

Do you agree with this assessment? Makes notes for and against the above proposition. Then write a concluding paragraph, summarising your own view.

- Cordelia is a figure of constant virtue, who shows her integrity in the love-test, yet still does all she can to support her father when he is overthrown.
- Cordelia's death turns her into a passive martyr-like figure.
- Regan and Goneril are two-faced villains who will do anything to satisfy their appetites. Both connive at Gloucester's torture. Regan kills the servant who stabs Cornwall; Goneril poisons Regan, tells Oswald to kill Gloucester and plans to have her husband Albany killed.
- However, it can be argued that their dynamism and determination raise Regan and Goneril above mere stereotypes.
- Cordelia is no passive heroine – she speaks up in the love-test and brings an army to rescue her father.

## Revision task 7: Ecocriticism

Anthony Parr has suggested that, given its attention to conflicting ideas of 'nature', *King Lear* might be considered from an ecological perspective.

Make a list of moments in the play which could be interpreted from this point of view. For example, when Lear divides up the country for the love-test, he sees 'our kingdom' (I.1.37) purely as property which he can dispose of as he pleases, with no apparent regard for guardianship of the land or for the welfare of the creatures who reside there.

- Throughout the play nature is seen as a source of nourishment and support (for example, when Cordelia calls medicinal herbs the 'unpublished virtues of the earth', IV.4.16) – even the storm on the heath can be seen as nature's reaction against human evil.
- We see a dramatic contrast between Lear's idea of Britain as a map he can divide as he pleases, and Britain as a place where life has somehow to be lived by less privileged people like beggars and by the tenant who leads Gloucester at the start of Act IV.
- Edmund shares Lear's initial view that land is not a responsibility to be looked after but a means to power, declaring 'Legitimate Edgar, I must have your land' (I.2.16).
- Both Lear and Edmund question what nature is and how human nature relates to it.

- Edmund rejects the traditional view of nature's influence on human behaviour as superstition and an 'evasion of whoremaster man' (I.2.130–1) – but takes responsibility for his own behaviour only so that he can behave in a wholly unnatural and irresponsible way.

## Revision task 8: Tragedy

Write a paragraph explaining what makes Lear a tragic figure. Are there any other characters who might be regarded as tragic? If so, do the same for them, noting how their situation is similar to – or different from – Lear's situation.

- Lear's arrogant and irresponsible division of the kingdom brings about his downfall, yet his punishment seems far in excess of his crime and it is possible that he behaved as he did precisely because he sensed his mind was failing.
- Lear does not suffer passively, but learns from his experiences, seeing reality more clearly and understanding something of his own responsibility for past errors.
- Lear's 'madness' is an affliction but also a transforming experience through which he is able to progress to a new sense of identity and values.
- Above all, Lear learns to appreciate Cordelia, and his unsuccessful attempt to save her life and his final grief over her dead body bring his story to a terrible conclusion.
- Gloucester is also punished excessively for a bad error of judgement and learns to love the faithful child that he had rejected – but he is plunged into suicidal despair and does not show Lear's heroism.

## Revision task 9: Plot and subplot

Draw up a chart so that you can see clearly how the main plot and subplot interact. One way to do this would be to draw three columns and go through the play scene by scene, putting the story of Lear and his daughters in one, that of Gloucester and his sons in another and their overlap in the third. Do you see a pattern emerge?

*Possible points to include:*

- Lear rejects Cordelia and hands over his power to Goneril and Regan; Gloucester rejects Edgar and names Edmund his successor.
- Lear has a mental breakdown in the storm, where he takes shelter with Edgar, who is pretending to be mad.
- Lear is so ashamed of what he has done that he is reluctant to meet with Cordelia; Edgar is unwilling to reveal himself to Gloucester, perhaps because he is upset at his treatment, perhaps because he has lost faith in his father's discretion.
- Lear and Cordelia are reunited and Lear tries unsuccessfully to save Cordelia from murder; Edgar saves Gloucester from suicide and from Oswald's murder attempt, then reveals himself to his father, who is overcome and dies.
- There are strong parallels between the plot and subplot: by Act V Edmund, Goneril and Regan have become the villains in both plots, while Edgar has become the hero and Cordelia the heroine. Tate's 1681 rewrite of the play in which Edgar and Cordelia finally marry has a strong narrative logic therefore – which may be one reason why Shakespeare's decision to kill off Cordelia still has the power to shock.

# PROGRESS CHECK ANSWERS

## Part Two: Studying *King Lear*

### Section One: Check your understanding

**1.** How far in your view is Lear responsible for his own downfall?

- Lear banishes his loyal daughter Cordelia and counsellor Kent.
- He gives power to Goneril and Regan, who merely flatter him.
- His behaviour in retirement is irresponsible and confrontational.
- He may be suffering from senility, so not be entirely responsible.
- The main responsibility lies with Regan and Goneril, who take advantage of his weaknesses.

**2.** How does Shakespeare seek to place Cordelia in a good light about her attitude to Lear and the invasion of Britain?

- Cordelia's asides show us that she is not malicious, but in a difficult situation.
- Kent and the King of France assure us that Cordelia's behaviour has been reasonable.
- The insincerity of Goneril and Regan puts Cordelia in a good light.
- Cordelia's arrival is depicted as a rescue mission, not a French invasion.
- Having lost the battle, Cordelia is brave and stoical.

**3.** What precisely are Goneril and Regan's complaints about their father? How far do you sympathise with them?

- They say that Lear is confrontational and quarrelsome.
- His followers, too, are 'riotous' (I.3.7) and a burden to accommodate.
- Since Lear has given them 'all' (II.4.249), their complaints are disproportionate.
- Our sympathy depends on how Lear and his followers are seen to behave on stage.

**4.** How does the Duke of Kent contribute to the development of the story?

- He makes clear Lear's folly in the first scene.
- By returning in disguise, he shows us how Lear can inspire loyalty.
- He escalates Lear's confrontation with Goneril, Regan and Cornwall.
- He gives us news of Cordelia's return.
- He reminds everyone of Lear's absence in the final scene.

**5.** Break down the stages of Lear's 'madness'.

- His judgement is unsound in the first scene, which may imply senility.
- His arguments with Goneril and Regan show alarming mood swings and lack of self-control.
- In the storm he is overcome by emotion and fears he is losing his mind.
- Therafter 'his wits begin t'unsettle' (III.4.163) and he becomes irrational and obsessive.
- He recovers after a long sleep at Cordelia's camp, but is finally traumatised by Cordelia's death.

**6.** How does Edmund convince Gloucester that Edgar is plotting against him?

- He forges an incriminating letter, which he pretends he is trying to conceal.
- He appears to defend Edgar while suggesting the letter does reflect his views.
- He persuades Edgar to behave suspiciously by going into hiding.
- He stages a fight with Edgar and cuts himself to pretend that Edgar attacked him.
- He lies that Edgar tried to make him agree they should kill Gloucester.

**7.** Some critics consider Goneril and Regan virtually interchangeable. Make notes on any differences between them which you can find.

- Goneril more often takes the initiative, e.g. in the love-test and the conversation afterwards.
- Regan encourages her husband to do evil. Goneril uses Oswald to assist her and plots to kill her unco-operative husband.
- Further differences will be created by the performance of the actors.

**8.** What is the Fool trying to make Lear realise?

- Lear is foolish ('Thou should'st not have been old till thou hadst been wise', I.5.40–1).
- He has put his daughters in control and now has no power ('thou mad'st thy daughters thy mothers', I.4.169–70).
- He has reduced himself to 'nothing' (I.4.192).

**9.** List five questions that Lear asks during the play and comment on what they reveal about him.

- 'Which of you shall we say doth love us most?' (I.1.50) – Lear prefers praise to truth, and confuses political decisions and personal relationships.
- 'Who is it that can tell me who I am?' (I.4.228) – Lear's sarcasm unintentionally reveals the way that his changing role has undermined his sense of identity.
- 'How dost, my boy? Art cold?' (III.2.68) – Lear's concern for the Fool shows he can rise above his own troubles and think of others.
- 'Is man no more than this?' (III.4.104–5) – Seeing Poor Tom, Lear casts aside his pretensions and reflects on what is most basic in human nature.
- 'Why should a dog, a horse, a rat, have life, / And thou no breath at all?' (V.3.306–7) – Lear faces up to the mystery of life and death.

**10.** Why is the storm scene (Act III Scene 1) important? What would be lost if it was removed?

- The storm symbolises the upheaval in Lear's life, his family and the state.
- It gives dramatic expression to Lear's rejection, showing how exposed and helpless he is.
- Without the sublime raging of the elements, Lear's story would seem more of a family quarrel, less of a reflection on humanity's place in nature.

**11.** Choose three soliloquies and make notes on what the audience learns from them.

*For example, III.6.101–14:*

- We are reminded that Poor Tom is really Edgar, who is still sane and thoughtful.
- He emphasises how dreadful it is to see the king, the nation's leader, suffer such a breakdown.
- He draws our attention to the parallel between the plot and subplot.
- He indicates that he is not merely hiding, but intends to seek justice.

**12.** Sum up the differences between Lear and Edmund's views of nature.

- Lear initially assumes there is a divine order in nature, which is also expressed in society's hierarchy and values.
- Edmund thinks society and morality have no basis in nature and life is just a battle for dominance.
- Lear comes to question his ideas about nature once his life falls apart.

**13.** Find three references to the pagan gods and comment on how an audience might respond to each of them.

- Lear swears by Apollo in Act I Scene 1 but fails to intimidate Kent. A Christian audience would regard Lear's oath as empty and side with Kent.
- Edgar proclaims, 'The Gods are just' for causing his father to be blinded as punishment for his adultery (V.3.170). These are harsh, unchristian sentiments and an audience would probably reject them, yet have some sympathy for Edgar's feelings.
- When Cordelia calls upon the 'kind Gods' to heal her father (IV.7.14), an audience will sympathise, but perhaps reflect that all the references to the gods tell us about the speakers' feelings, not whether the gods of any religion exist.

**14.** What is the symbolic importance of sight in the play?

- From the first scene, sight is used metaphorically to refer to good or bad judgement.
- Gloucester's blinding is symbolically equivalent to Lear's madness.
- Gloucester 'sees' life more clearly when he has no eyes, just as Lear becomes more perceptive when he loses his mind.

**15.** Draw up a table showing resemblances between the main plot of Lear and his daughters, and the subplot of Gloucester and his sons.

*Possible points to include:*

- Lear rejects Cordelia and hands over his power to Goneril and Regan; Gloucester rejects Edgar and names Edmund his successor.
- Lear is afflicted by mental ill health, Gloucester by blindness – each a symbolically appropriate punishment for poor judgement.
- Lear and Cordelia are reunited and Lear tries unsuccessfully to save Cordelia from murder; Edgar and Gloucester are reunited and Edgar does save Gloucester from suicide and murder, though Gloucester dies shortly after.

**16.** Write down at least three examples of how the play shows the rich and powerful in a critical light.

- Lear divides up the country with no apparent concern for the way the change of leader will affect the inhabitants.

- In the storm, Lear realises that his plight is shared by many homeless 'naked wretches' (III.4.28) and that as king he has not supported them.
- Once he has learned to question authority, Lear realises that the poor cannot hide their sins while the rich escape the supposedly 'strong lance of justice' (IV.6.164).

**17.** How does Albany change during the course of the play?

- In Act I Scene 4 he is perplexed by the confrontation between Goneril and Lear.
- By Act IV Scene 2 he realises Goneril's evil, expresses hatred for her and promises to take revenge for Gloucester's blinding.
- He fights Cordelia's army to prevent a foreign invasion, but once this is accomplished he arrests Edmund and seizes control from Goneril and Regan.

**18.** The cuts made in the Folio version of the play include the mock trial of Act III Scene 6 and all of Act IV Scene 3. What is lost if these two episodes are removed and do you think these losses damage the play?

- Act III Scene 6 lets us see Gloucester and Edgar supporting Lear.
- Act IV Scene 3 prepares us for the reunion of Lear and Cordelia by telling us how they feel about one another.
- Our understanding of and sympathy for all of these characters is slightly diminished by the cuts.

**19.** Kent and Edgar remain in disguise until the last scene. Would it have been possible for them to reveal their identities earlier? And if so, why do they not do so?

- Both characters are likely to be in serious danger if their identities are found out before order is restored.
- Kent has less to fear than Edgar but claims an unnamed 'dear cause' prevents him revealing himself (IV.3.51). Perhaps he is spying on the usurpers' army; perhaps Shakespeare does not want to break the momentum of the story.
- By delaying Edgar's revelation until he has defeated Edmund, Shakespeare is able to make it a moment of dramatic triumph and establish Edgar as a character who is welcomed and admired by all, ready for his transition to ruler.

**20.** How do Edgar's experiences help him gain qualities which may be beneficial to him as a king?

- Edgar has learned self-control and wariness in trusting others.
- He has learned to be patient but to act decisively when the right moment comes.
- He has come to understand the needs of the poor and afflicted, which Lear neglected.
- He has learned to act ruthlessly when necessary, even killing his own brother.
- He has persuaded himself that the gods support justice and are on his side.

## Section Two: Working towards the exam

**1.** 'King Lear gives us a totally pessimistic picture of the human condition.' Do you agree?

- Certainly bleak, as Jan Kott argues, with families turning against one another and a large number of characters dying before their time.

- Lear and Gloucester come to see that society is unjust and hypocritical, but they themselves can do nothing to change it.
- Lear and Gloucester learn humility and the value of love, but are reunited with their loved ones for a pitifully short time.
- The most innocent character, Cordelia, is wantonly murdered.
- Yet the forces of evil are defeated, and it is Lear and Gloucester's behaviour that helps to bring about their own downfall.
- Edgar's suffering has prepared him to create a comparatively just order.
- The play should not be described as pessimistic simply because it does not give us the naïve happy ending of a popular film; it might be fairer to call it very guardedly optimistic.

**2.** Despite its tragic subject, *King Lear* is a gripping, suspenseful work of drama. Choose an extract from the play and analyse how dramatic interest is maintained.

*For example, V.3.41–91:*

- Edmund has just arranged to have Lear and Cordelia murdered and throughout the scene we await news of the outcome, hoping they will be saved.
- The suspense increases when Edmund and Albany quarrel over access to the prisoners.
- Attention shifts to Goneril and Regan's dispute over Edmund, with a first hint that Regan has been poisoned, confirmed by Goneril's aside a few lines later.
- Albany adds further drama by arresting Edmund and Goneril and reminding us of the disguised Edgar's challenge.
- We then become so engaged with the forthcoming fight that we cease to think of Lear and Cordelia, until Kent's arrival suddenly reminds us.

**3.** In what ways does *King Lear* illustrate the idea that power corrupts?

- Lear behaves tyrannically in Act I Scene 1.
- When he loses power, he comes to recognise the hypocrisy of the strong punishing the weak.
- Once Regan and Goneril gain power, they embrace corruption, culminating in Goneril's poisoning of her sister.
- Released from Lear's control, Cornwall blinds Gloucester.
- However, power does not corrupt Albany, and Edmund is evil before he gains power.
- The play suggests that Edgar's experience of poverty and rejection may protect him from the corrupting effects of power.

**4.** To what extent do you agree that Lear achieves redemption through suffering?

- Lear is guilty of several harmful deeds in Act I Scene 1.
- His 'madness' involves a breakdown of his royal persona.
- He comes to see the hypocrisy and tyranny which hierarchy encourages.
- Applying this perception to himself, he is humbled and learns that his relationship with Cordelia is the most important thing in his life.
- He kills her murderer and dies with a full appreciation of her worth.
- Cordelia's remark that she is going about her father's business (IV.4.23–4) suggests she is a Christ-like figure.
- Nonetheless, the play is set in pagan times and Lear cannot have been redeemed in the Christian sense.

**5.** A tragic hero is often defined as an important person who suffers a colossal downfall, partly through a flaw in their character, whose experiences show us the capacities and limits of human life. How well does this definition apply to Lear?

- As king, Lear is of supreme importance and his downfall leaves the country exposed to the tyranny of Goneril, Regan and Cornwall, as well as foreign invasion.
- He falls into mental instability and vagrancy, ending as an old man cared for by others.
- His flaws include poor judgement and arrogance.
- His humiliation, breakdown and death show some of life's most terrible constraints, to which may be added the blinding of Gloucester and the death of Cordelia.
- The capacities of life can be seen in Lear's ability to learn, change and engage heroically with life until the end.
- The definition applies well, though Lear is distinctive as a tragic hero who actually grows in stature in the later part of the play.

# Part Three: Characters and themes

## Section One: Check your understanding

**1.** List the ways in which Lear's love-test might be considered irrational and irresponsible.

- He has already decided beforehand who will get which part of the country.
- He knows that Goneril and Regan's husbands are rivals who may use their new power divisively.
- He knows Cordelia is likely to marry a foreign ruler, who may meddle in British affairs.
- By banishing Cordelia and Kent, he puts himself at the mercy of Goneril and Regan.

**2.** How thoroughly does Edmund reject the social hierarchy? Write a paragraph assessing his attitude.

- His first soliloquy (II.1) states that laws and rules are artificial barriers to merit.
- Nonetheless, he wishes to rise in the hierarchy, not destroy it.
- At his death, he makes his peace with the social system, praising Edgar's nobility and trying to behave in a way of which others would approve.

**3.** How does the animal imagery which is applied to Goneril and Regan shape our view of them?

- 'Wolfish visage' (I.4.305) – Lear describes Goneril as a predatory animal and hopes Regan will fight her. Ironically, he chooses an animal that hunts in packs: he will soon find them attacking him together.
- 'Pelican daughters' (III.4.76) – it was mistakenly thought that pelicans ate their parents' flesh, so Lear is expressing his fear of what they may do to him.
- 'Tigers' (IV.2.40) – Albany describes them as ferocious, unstoppable predators.

**4.** List reasons which might account for the Fool's disappearance after Act III Scene 6.

- He may have got separated from Lear's group.

- He may have reluctantly decided to abandon Lear because he was on a course of self-destruction.
- Lear's plight is so well established that Shakespeare no longer needs the Fool to emphasise it.
- If the same actor played the Fool and Cordelia, he would have to concentrate on the second role now.

**5.** Write a paragraph on how Albany changes during the course of the play.

- He is perplexed by the confrontation between Goneril and Lear, and fails to intervene in time. His loyalty to Goneril seems to inhibit him.
- He later realises Goneril's evil, expresses hatred for her and promises to take revenge for Gloucester's blinding.
- Now energised, he fights Cordelia's army to prevent a foreign invasion, but once this is accomplished he arrests Edmund, seizes control from Goneril and Regan, and concludes the play by giving power to Edgar.

**6.** Summarise in a couple of paragraphs the importance of clothing and nudity in the play.

- Clothing is often associated with misleading appearance. The well-dressed nobles often behave more shabbily than their servants.
- Kent has to adopt a servant's costume in order to be able to do good.
- When Edgar and Lear remove their clothes, it symbolises discarding the inessential and finding out about their real selves.

**7.** Find three examples of different ways in which the word 'nothing' is used and comment on them.

- Cordelia's 'Nothing, my Lord' (I.1.86) is a refusal to compromise herself by taking part in the demeaning love-test.
- Lear's 'Nothing will come of nothing' (I.1.89) is a threat to Cordelia, based on his power as king to either award wealth and power or withhold them.
- The Fool's 'thou art nothing' (I.4.192) is a blunt statement to Lear of what he becomes when he gives up the power by which he defined himself.

**8.** Why do you think so many people have been shocked by the death of Cordelia? Give three reasons.

- She did not die in previous versions of the story.
- She is the embodiment of virtue and hope.
- With the defeat of Edmund, Regan and Goneril, the play seems to be moving to a positive resolution, so for Cordelia to die at this point is particularly distressing.

**9.** The Folio version of the play omits Lear's mock trial of Goneril and Regan. Write a paragraph discussing what might be lost by its removal.

- It gives additional shape to the play by parodying the love-test, so emphasising Lear's diminished power and increased understanding.
- Its black humour forms a dramatic contrast to the blinding of Gloucester in the next scene.
- It gives us a sustained view both of Lear's 'madness' and Edgar's feigned instability.

**10.** Give three examples of how the characters' references to the gods are undermined.

- When Lear swears by Apollo, Kent derides it as 'in vain' (I.1.160).
- Lear calls on 'you Gods' (II.4.271) for noble anger, but it does not prevent him from weeping.
- Edgar declares, 'The Gods are just' (V.3.170), shortly before we learn of Cordelia's death.

### Section Two: Working towards the exam

**1.** How sympathetic a character do you find Lear? How might an audience's response to him change during the course of the play?

- He seems to be a vain tyrant in Act I Scene 1.
- His treatment by Goneril and his toleration of the Fool's mockery make us more sympathetic to him.
- When Regan and Goneril strip him of his followers and he breaks down, we are bound to have some feeling for his suffering.
- During his breakdown he undergoes a transformation – his willingness to confront uncomfortable truths intrigues us.
- His new relationship with Cordelia, from his contrition to his heroic attempt to save her life, arouses total sympathy.
- Overall, we feel increasing sympathy without ever quite forgetting that he bears significant responsibility for his own afflictions.

**2.** Explore the differences and similarities we see in the characters of Edmund and Edgar.

- On the first two occasions we see them together, Edmund is cunningly manipulative and Edgar 'so far from doing harms / That he suspects none' (I.2.184–5).
- If we sympathise with Edmund's resentment against Edgar, this fades as we see how Edmund mistreats him.
- Disguising himself as Poor Tom, Edgar shows he can be equally as cunning as Edmund.
- Edmund has no compunction about betraying his father, whereas Edgar, who has good reason to be angry with Gloucester, still does his best to help him.
- Edmund does not attack Gloucester or Edgar in person, but Edgar is determined to kill his brother in single combat.
- Both brothers are capable of ruthless cunning in order to assert their interests – Edgar also possesses a conscience and sense of duty that make him a hero.

**3.** It has been said that *King Lear* is a play in which madness leads to greater understanding of the truth. To what extent do you agree with this observation?

- Lear has spent a lifetime being flattered and getting his own way.
- The breakdown he experiences enables him to see society and himself afresh.
- Gloucester is equally complacent about his wisdom and security.
- His blinding plunges him into a depression, but enables him to question his assumptions and fully appreciate Edgar.
- Edgar plays the role of a 'madman' which helps to change his personality, becoming more cunning and ruthless.
- Inhabiting the world of the destitute and fighting for survival teach Edgar lessons about society and power which will be of value to him as a king.

# Part Four: Genre, structure and language

## Section One: Check your understanding

**1.** A tragedy commonly includes reversals of fortune and moments of discovery. Find three examples of each and comment on the audience's likely reactions to them.

- Reversals of fortune include King Lear becoming homeless and unwell, the Earl of Kent becoming the servant Caius, and Edmund becoming Earl of Gloucester.
- Moments of discovery include the announcement that Cordelia is returning with an army, Goneril's aside that she has poisoned Regan, and Lear's entry carrying Cordelia's dead body.
- Each reversal of fortune is shocking and makes us want to know what will happen next to the character concerned; each moment of discovery represents a major step in the unfolding of the story and makes us evaluate its implications.

**2.** Write a couple of paragraphs comparing Lear and Gloucester as tragic figures.

- Flawed judgement causes their downfall – Lear rejects Cordelia and gives power to his other daughters; Gloucester rejects Edgar and says he will make Edmund his successor.
- Lear is afflicted by 'madness', Gloucester by blindness – each a symbolically appropriate punishment for their poor judgement.
- Lear is reunited with Cordelia and tries unsuccessfully to save her from being killed; Gloucester is reunited with Edgar but dies shortly after.

**3.** Lear's flaw (or hamartia) has been described as arrogance, overvaluation of appearance, lack of self-knowledge and lack of self-control. Write a paragraph explaining your own view of his weakness.

- Lear fails to distinguish between himself as a person and his role as king.
- This makes him arrogant and complacent about others' respect for him.
- When he is treated badly, he thinks wrongly that he can still intimidate people with a display of bad temper.

**4.** If you had to divide the play into three sections, separated by two intervals, where would you place the breaks and why?

*There is no correct answer, but the three sections should be of roughly comparable size.*

- The end of Act II Scene 2, when Kent is in the stocks and Edgar on the run, would be an appropriate moment for the audience to reflect on the rise of the evil characters and what might happen next.
- The end of Act IV Scene 2 would emphasise a muted sense of hope, as Edgar agrees to lead the blinded Gloucester to Dover, where Lear is also being taken.

**5.** Note three occasions where the noble characters switch to prose and for each example suggest why Shakespeare might have made that decision.

- Gloucester and Kent open the play by gossiping about sordid matters.

- Kent uses prose to abuse Oswald in Act II Scene 2.
- In contrast to these examples of 'low' subject matter, Gloucester speaks in prose in Act III Scene 3, apparently because he is preoccupied and agitated.

**6.** Find five asides in the play and suggest why each was included.

- Cordelia's asides in the first scene show us that her motives for defying her father are pure ones.
- Edgar's comment in the mock trial (III.6.60–1) reminds us that his role as Poor Tom is a pretence and shows us his sympathy for Lear.
- Goneril's reaction to the death of Cornwall shows us she is now scheming against her sister (IV.2.83–7).
- Edgar explains why he subjects his father to the cliff trick (IV.6.33–4) so that the audience do not think he is being spiteful.
- Goneril's reaction to Regan's sickness (V.3.97) makes it clear that she is responsible for poisoning her.

**7.** Look at how the word 'nothing' is used in the play and write a paragraph summing up its significance.

- Cordelia's 'Nothing, my Lord' (I.1.86) is a refusal to endorse the love-test.
- Lear's 'Nothing will come of nothing' (I.1.89) is a threat to Cordelia, based on his power to award or withhold wealth and power.
- The Fool's 'thou art nothing' (I.4.192) is a blunt statement to Lear of what he becomes when he gives up the power by which he defined himself.
- Recurring throughout the play, the word has a thematic resonance in a story about how much loss an individual can withstand and still retain their identity and sense of life as meaningful.

**8.** Copy or print out a key speech, such as Lear's 'Blow, winds' (III.2.1–9), and annotate it, advising the actor on how the lines should best be spoken.

- Strongly emphasise the verbs to show the force of Lear's feelings: 'Blow … crack … rage … blow … spout … drenched' and so on.
- Pause significantly after 'singe my white head!' as if he really believes the lightning will come at his instruction.
- Lower your tone and voice as you reach 'ingrateful man' to show Lear's present contempt for humankind.

**9.** Look at how the words 'nature' and 'natural' are used in the play. List as many different meanings of them as you can find and note who uses them in which contexts.

- Lear and Gloucester use 'nature' to refer to a divinely-ordained order of right and wrong, to which people should conform.
- Edmund uses the word in the same way when he wishes to deceive, but when sincere he uses it to refer to the material world and its natural competition for survival and dominance.
- Characters often refer to an individual's 'nature' or personality, the desires of which may or may not be aligned with the supposed divine order.

**10.** On stage, words and actions go together. Open the play at random and make notes on what movements, gestures and expressions the actor might make in delivering the lines that you find there.

*For example, Act III Scene 3:*

- Gloucester paces about in agitation, going up to Edmund for his second speech in order to speak to him in a private, intimate way.
- Edmund follows him onto the stage but holds himself aloof, keeping calm, perhaps even amused by his father's distress.
- After Gloucester's departure, Edmund speaks his first two lines in his direction, then steps to the front and confides the last three to the audience.

## Section Two: Working towards the exam

**1.** 'Without the subplot of Gloucester and his sons, *King Lear* would be a much poorer play.' To what extent do you agree?

- The theme of 'blindness' to the truth is much clearer for being enacted through both Lear and Gloucester.
- Movement between the two plots adds considerable variety to the dramatic experience.
- This movement also enables each plot to move at a variable speed, with a few minutes or a few days passing in the interim.
- A sense is created that the themes do not apply to one family only, but have a wider application. The rivalry between Edgar and Edmund gives us a traditional struggle between good and evil, which gives the play strong narrative momentum.
- The rivalry brings a positive element to the play's conclusion when Edgar wins and becomes king.

**2.** How do the comic elements in the play support the tragedy, rather than detract from it?

- The Fool's witticisms constantly challenge Lear to admit to his folly.
- Kent's pursuit of Oswald round the stage at the start of Act II Scene 2 releases tension by letting us see a temporary victory of good over evil.
- The mock trial in the hovel shows us Lear's feelings and also his inability to enact them in reality.
- Albany's plain-speaking to Goneril in Act IV Scene 2 gives us the satisfaction of hearing her evil named aloud by someone in a position to resist her.
- In the final meeting between Lear and Gloucester, moments of comic behaviour throw into relief the horror and sadness of the two men's positions.
- Albany's assertion that Edmund cannot marry Regan because he is engaged to his own wife Goneril, shows us the confidence with which Albany is taking charge.

**3.** '*King Lear* is a tragedy of political power, but also a family tragedy.' Discuss.

- The tragedy begins with Lear's misconceived attempt to manage the succession to the throne.
- Power rivalry between his elder daughters and their husbands lies behind the ill-treatment of Lear and Gloucester.
- Rivalry between Edmund and Edgar for succession to the earldom leads to their mortal conflict.
- Britain is put in danger of civil war and of having rulers with no respect for legality.
- Lear is a bad father, who has alienated Goneril and Regan and learns respect for Cordelia when it is almost too late; Gloucester shows little understanding of his sons and their feelings.
- Lear's family all die in the last scene.

## Part Five: Contexts and interpretations

### Section One: Check your understanding

**1.** List three aspects of Shakespeare's plays that might be considered characteristic of the Renaissance.

- They implicitly question social assumptions, including religion and the divine right of kings.
- They often feature Machiavellian villains.
- They take a keen interest in the state of the nation.

**2.** Choose several scenes from *King Lear* and note, in the absence of scenery, what clues the audience would have about where each one is set.

*For example:*

- II.2 – Oswald's references to 'this house' and stabling facilities indicate the scene takes place outside Gloucester's house; the rapid arrival of the nobles shows it is very near the main building.
- III.2 – the location is indicated by the Gentleman's speech in the previous scene; Lear and Kent both describe the weather conditions vividly; Kent alerts us to the hovel.
- V.1 – We are told in the previous scene that a battle is imminent; soldiers and flags show us that this is a British army camp; Edmund and Albany address one another as though they have just rendezvoused to prepare for the fight.

**3.** Note three features of the play which are typical of the generation of playwrights to which Shakespeare belonged.

- It is in blank verse.
- It is secular, rather than religious, in theme.
- It based on history and legend.

**4.** Draw a rough plan of the Globe stage and make notes on how a scene of your choice might be staged to appeal to an audience on three sides.

*For Act III Scene 2, possible points to include:*

- Lear would prowl around the front of the stage, going from side to side, shouting his defiance to the storm, while the Fool hangs back behind him.
- Kent enters and advances to Lear, then follows him in his agitated progress to and fro.
- When they leave, the Fool comes to the front and addresses the audience, turning and looking around the theatre to take them all in.

**5.** What are the major contrasts between the opening scene at court and the final scene at Dover?

- The opening takes place inside the king's palace; the ending is outdoors beside a battlefield, with the characters exposed to the elements.
- Lear presides over the court as a figure of total authority; Lear is a released prisoner, confused and overcome, and dies on the bare ground.
- The royal family are placed in senior positions and do most of the talking; the royal family are under others' control and all die, two by murder, one by suicide – only Lear by a 'natural' death.
- Kent is dressed as an earl and speaks up strongly; Kent is dressed as a servant and is little more than a bystander.

- Albany scarcely speaks, Edgar is absent; Albany and Edgar are in charge.

**6.** How do the scenes set in Gloucester's residence show the shifting balance of power, and the immoral nature of Lear's opponents?

- Edmund lies to Gloucester to make him turn against Edgar and make Edmund his heir.
- Cornwall and Regan take over the residence, putting Kent in the stocks against Gloucester's judgement.
- They shut the door against Lear and forbid Gloucester to help him.
- They torture Gloucester, putting out both his eyes.

**7.** List the main faults found in *King Lear* by critics prior to the twentieth century.

- The ending is gratuitously unjust and depressing.
- The subplot of Gloucester and his sons is unbelievable and a distraction from the main plot.
- The evil behaviour of the villains is too extreme to be credible.
- The blinding scene is too horrible to stage and much of the play works better on the page than in the theatre.

**8.** Do you agree that comedy is an essential part of the play, as G. Wilson Knight suggests? Would the tragedy be less effective if it was removed?

- Wilson Knight argued for the importance of the comic element, which he felt enhanced the tragedy.
- This seems to be a paradox, as you might expect humour to dilute the tragic atmosphere.
- In practice, a constant tragic tone would become monotonous and lose effect, so comic elements like the Fool's wit and some of the incongruous dialogue in the 'mad' scenes add a helpful variety.

**9.** How convincing do you find the arguments for and against *King Lear* being a Christian play?

- Cordelia is a Christ-like figure in her integrity, forgiveness and death at the hands of her enemies. Her speech contains an allusion to Jesus (IV.4.23–4).
- Lear and Edgar both learn humility, but not forgiveness or turning the other cheek – both kill an opponent in the last scene.
- The play is set in pagan times, so Lear cannot be 'redeemed' in a Christian sense.
- It can be argued that the play depicts pagans, but that some of their values correspond to Christian ones, particularly in the case of Cordelia.
- It can also be argued that Shakespeare uses the pagan setting to cast doubt on whether there is any divine order except in people's minds.

**10.** How does Jonathan Dollimore's view of Lear contrast with A. C. Bradley's?

- For Bradley, the play is about Lear's self-discovery – suffering enables the king to come to terms with his true nature.
- For Dollimore, the play is about power – how its redistribution after Lear steps down has a shattering effect on society's structure.
- In Dollimore's reading, Lear's breakdown is caused by the loss of his established roles and status.

**Section Two: Working towards the exam**

**1.** To what extent might the play be considered to challenge received ideas of gender?

- The plays begins at a patriarchal court where the female members of the royal family are required to flatter the ultimate male authority, their father.
- Cordelia rebels in a measured way – her sisters pretend to comply, then rebel in an extreme way in reaction to past repression.
- Lear rejects dominance by his daughters, and even tries to suppress his emotions and tears, which he thinks of as female in nature.
- Eventually, Lear rejects male dominance and repression, and briefly achieves an authentic love with Cordelia.
- An alternative view is that Regan and Goneril are a lesson in what happens if women are allowed too much power.
- Cordelia, in contrast to her sisters' lust for evil, becomes a submissive heroine.
- Each view can be supported from the text – how the play is acted may be the chief determinant.

**2.** 'For Lear the journey from his palace to Dover is a tragic fall, but for Edgar the same journey is a learning experience that prepares him for kingship.' Discuss.

- Lear begins as a king, becomes a dependent, then an itinerant 'madman' and finally a prisoner, before dying with the body of his youngest daughter in his arms.
- Although it can be argued that Lear gains spiritual benefits from this journey, it indisputably represents a tragic fall.
- Edgar begins as the heir to the earldom of Gloucester, becomes a fugitive, then adopts the identity of an itinerant madman, leads his father and saves him from murder only to have him die in his arms, then kills his own brother.
- Edgar's journey is similar to Lear's, but crucially Edgar only pretends to be mad – his radical disguise enables him to elude capture and adopt a strategy of patience.
- Having correctly judged the moment to strike, Edgar successfully kills his tormentor (Edmund).
- It is too late for Lear to start again – but Edgar's knowledge of rich and poor, his patience and his ruthlessness equip him well to be a king.

**3.** 'Lear's identity is a social construction.' How far do you agree?

- Lear initially appears in his authoritarian roles of king and father.
- By Act I Scene 4 it is clear from Goneril and Oswald's behaviour towards him that Lear can no longer sustain either role, eroding his sense of identity – 'This is not Lear' (I.4.224).
- By Act II Scene 4 his daughters' denial of his authority causes a breakdown of his personality.
- This process enables him to realise how much he has depended on a false view of himself created by flatterers – 'they told me I was every thing' (IV.6.104–5).
- He comes to accept a less imposing identity – 'I am a very foolish fond old man' (IV.7.60).
- Yet Cordelia continues to love him as her father and loyal subjects like Kent still give him the respect due to a king.
- Arguably, everyone's identity is a social construct and Lear's is one strongly rooted in reality. He begins the play with a grandiose view of himself, but it is exaggerated rather than false.

# MARK SCHEME

Use this page to assess your answer to the **Practice task** on page 108.

Look at the elements listed for each Assessment Objective. Examiners will be looking to award the highest grades to the students who meet the majority of these criteria. If you can meet two to three elements from each AO, you are working at a good level, with some room for improvement to a higher level.*

> **'The main impression left on the audience at the end of *King Lear* is that after all the suffering there is little consolation.'**
>
> **By considering Shakespeare's dramatic methods, to what extent do you agree with this view?**

| | | |
|---|---|---|
| **A01** | Articulate informed, personal and creative responses to literary texts, using associated concepts and terminology, and coherent, accurate written expression. | • You make a range of clear, relevant points about tragic features.<br>• You use a range of literary terms correctly, e.g. **absurd, denouement, irony, tragedy**.<br>• You write a clear introduction, outlining your thesis and provide a clear conclusion.<br>• You signpost and link your ideas fluently about suffering and consolation within the play.<br>• You offer an overall personal interpretation or conceptualisation of the text which is well argued and convincing. |
| **A02** | Analyse ways in which meanings are shaped in literary texts. | • You explain the techniques and methods Shakespeare uses to present suffering.<br>• You explain in detail how such examples shape meaning, e.g. how Lear's mental breakdown throws up insights.<br>• You comment on how the dialogue between Lear and Cordelia in the final Act represents a rekindled relationship. |
| **A03** | Demonstrate understanding of the significance and influence of the contexts in which literary texts are written and received. | • You demonstrate your understanding of tragic terms and motifs – the 'hero' with a weakness that brings him down; the idea of hubris; the way events combine inexorably to bring about tragedy.<br>• Literary context: the tragedy genre.<br>• Historical context: divine right of kings. |
| **A04** | Explore connections across literary texts. | • You make relevant links between characters and ideas, noting how for example Lear and Gloucester are presented in the play. |
| **A05** | Explore literary texts informed by different interpretations. | • Where appropriate, you incorporate and comment on critics' views of the extent to which Lear can be seen as redeemed.<br>• You assert your own independent view clearly. |

*\* This mark scheme gives you a broad indication of attainment, but check the specific mark scheme for your paper/task to ensure you know what to focus on.*